The Earth

Oceans • Continents • Universe

Contents

PHENOMENA IN THE SKY 58

THREATS TO THE ENVIRONMENT 68

PLANET EARTH 76

THE UNIVERSE 86

APPENDIX 94

Inside the Earth

Until the 1950s most geologists believed that the earth had changed little since it was first formed more than 4.5 billion years ago. Recent research proves that the make-up of the earth is constantly changing. Thermodynamic processes, taking place in matter deep within the earth, change the appearance of our planet just as much as external factors such as the destruction of the environment, climate or cosmic rays.

We have an exact picture of how the continents came into existence: molten rock rose from the interior of the earth, which is partly liquid, and cooled on the surface. As it solidified, a crust of rock was formed. By a repeated process of melting and and resolidification, light rock was separated little by little from heavy rock to produce individual layers. In this way the continents were gradually formed. Volcanoes arose as a result of the great heat in the earth's interior. Their lava masses flowed out, thus providing the energy for the movement of the continents and the formation of mountain ranges. At the same time, the rock from eruptions gives us information about the earth's interior.

Data from earthquakes in particular allows us to draw conclusions about the structure of the earth's interior. By comparing measurements of the seismic waves it is possible to find out what type of material is involved as well as the location of rocks and natural resources. Other processes in the interior of the earth that can be observed from outside are its magnetic field and its temperature field.

The Structure of the Earth

150 years ago geologists differed widely in their opinions about what made up the interior of the earth. Some researchers believed that the inside of the earth consisted of a glowing ball of gas. Another group held the view that the earth is made of a number of layers, composed of various materials.

By collecting and examining rocks from different regions, geologists tried to find explanations for changes in the surface of the earth. As early as 1835 Sir Henry de la Beche (1796–1855) produced the first geological map of Great Britain. In the early 1990s a very deep hole was bored into the earth's crust in Germany. However, the project had to be stopped at a depth of 9,100 m, when drilling in brittle rock and, at the end, a malleable mass at 280 °C showed that even the most modern technology has its limits. On the Kola peninsula in the former Soviet Union engineers succeeded in drilling to a depth of 12,260 m.

There are also indirect ways of solving the mystery of the earth's interior. These include the investigation of seismic waves that result from explosions or earthquakes, or studying the earth's magnetic and gravitational fields.

Seismic waves are reflected deep inside the earth at places where there is a change in the type of rock, as well as at the transitions from the earth's crust to its mantle and core. The waves then return to the surface of the earth, where they can be recorded by seismographs. The speed of the waves and the depth at which they are reflected give us information about the interior of the earth. Today we know that the earth is surrounded by a crust consisting of relatively light rock. Below it is the earth's mantle, which is made up of solid stone on the outside and becomes molten towards the centre. Inside it is the core of the earth. A distinction is made between the inner and outer core, both of which probably consist largely of iron, with temperatures in the inner core probably reaching levels similar to those at the surface of the sun.

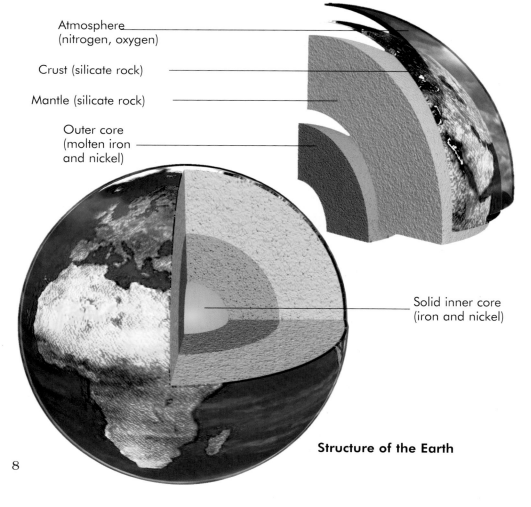

Atmosphere (nitrogen, oxygen)

Crust (silicate rock)

Mantle (silicate rock)

Outer core (molten iron and nickel)

Solid inner core (iron and nickel)

Structure of the Earth

The Earth's Crust

Our continents and the sea bed are on the outermost layer of the earth, the earth's crust. It is very thin in comparison to the radius of the earth, which is 6,370 km on average. Beneath the continents the crust is 20 to 100 km thick. Below Central Valley in California the earth's crust is only 20 km thick, but it has a thickness of up to 90 km beneath the Himalayas. Underneath the oceans the thickness of the crust ranges from 5 to 11 km. From the differences in the speed at which seismic waves travel, we conclude that there are different types of rock.

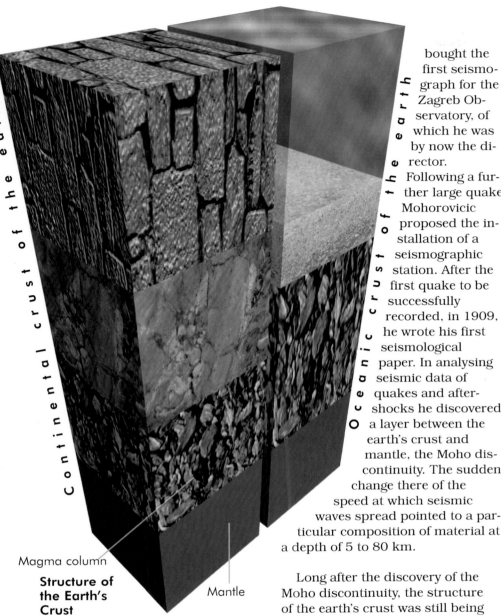

Continental crust of the earth

Oceanic crust of the earth

Magma column

Structure of the Earth's Crust

Mantle

bought the first seismograph for the Zagreb Observatory, of which he was by now the director.

Following a further large quake Mohorovicic proposed the installation of a seismographic station. After the first quake to be successfully recorded, in 1909, he wrote his first seismological paper. In analysing seismic data of quakes and aftershocks he discovered a layer between the earth's crust and mantle, the Moho discontinuity. The sudden change there of the speed at which seismic waves spread pointed to a particular composition of material at a depth of 5 to 80 km.

Long after the discovery of the Moho discontinuity, the structure of the earth's crust was still being examined by analysis of seismic waves. From the 1950s experiments were carried out with shock waves from explosions, which could be produced as desired at selected places and specified times. However, the energy of the waves penetrates only as far as the layers of the mantle. The continental crust is more varied and thicker than the oceanic crust. It contains rocks with an age of more than 4 billion years.

Erosion and deformation, uplift and subsidence have operated on it and produced a varied structure. Much of the surface is composed of sediments and volcanic rocks of low density. Below this is a folded, metamorphosed layer of sediment, adjacent to which – depending on the area – there is a granite layer. The deeper parts of the crust contain crystalline and metamorphosed rock layers extending as far as the mantle.

The structure of the oceanic crust is relatively simple. It is divided into just a few layers: lightly solidified sediment covers the surface. Its thickness ranges from a few hundred metres to three kilometres. The second layer consists of hard rock, containing mainly basalt but also a small proportion of sediment rock. It is 1.5 km thick on average. A third layer, approximately 5 km thick, has been investigated by deepwater drilling and consists mainly of the plutonic rock gabbro. Enormous columns of magma from the earth's mantle protrude into these layers.

The temperature inside the earth rises with increasing depth. The rise has been calculated as about 30 °C per km from the surface.

Between the crust and the mantle there is a clear boundary, known as the Mohorovicic discontinuity (Moho discontinuity for short). It is named after Andrija Mohorovicic, the Yugoslav seismologist who discovered it.

In 1887 Mohorovicic (1857–1936), originally a teacher of mathematics and physics, constructed a meteorological station and observed the frequent earthquakes in his locality with growing interest. In 1901, after the great earthquake in Zagreb, he

Oceanic Crust

Basalt

Continental Crust

Granite

The Earth's Mantle

Beneath the earth's crust lies the earth's mantle. It comprises 67% of the volume and 82% of the mass of the earth. Our information about its composition derives from seismic waves and volcanic emissions. The earth's mantle is relatively cool and has a density only one third higher than that of the continents. On the basis of its physical characteristics it can be divided into an upper and a lower layer.

The upper mantle consists of peridotite and basalts, among other materials. At depths between 100 and 200 km a change in the seismic waves takes place. This layer is known as the Gutenberg zone. Researchers believe that this reversal of the waves is the result of convection currents inside the earth. Together with the crust, the upper part of the mantle as far as the Gutenberg zone forms the lithosphere. Below it, and still belonging to the upper mantle, is the asthenosphere, in which the matter is less solid. It is involved in an exchange with the lithosphere. If matter from the asthenosphere rises at the mid-ocean ridge, it becomes part of the solid lithosphere. Conversely the ocean floors sink back into the earth's mantle at the edge of the continents (the so-called subduction zones) and are swallowed up there.

In the middle part of the mantle, which has a higher density, the speed of the seismic waves (P waves) also rises.

At a depth of about 2,900 km the lower mantle, which here consists mainly of silicate rock and has a density of 9.4 g/cm^3, borders on the earth's core. This region is called the Wiechert-Gutenberg discontinuity.

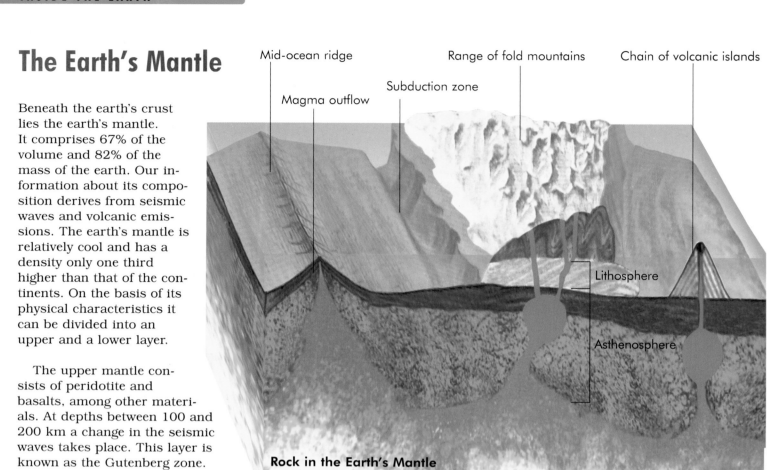

Mid-ocean ridge

Magma outflow

Subduction zone

Range of fold mountains

Chain of volcanic islands

Lithosphere

Asthenosphere

Rock in the Earth's Mantle

Mainly consolidated silicate rock

The Earth's Core

Relatively little is known about the core of the earth. Its distance from the earth's surface is thought to be about 2,900 km. However, this figure represents a highly inexact approximation, as researchers believe that the core of the earth is strongly asymmetrical. Seismic waves are able to pass through it only in part or are diverted by it.

Geologists have discovered that the outer core is probably molten, while the inner core is solid. Calculations of the density of the core put it four times higher than that of the crust.

As iron is the only element with this density, it probably constitutes the main part of the core, with nickel and also sulphur mixed in.

Molten core of nickel and iron

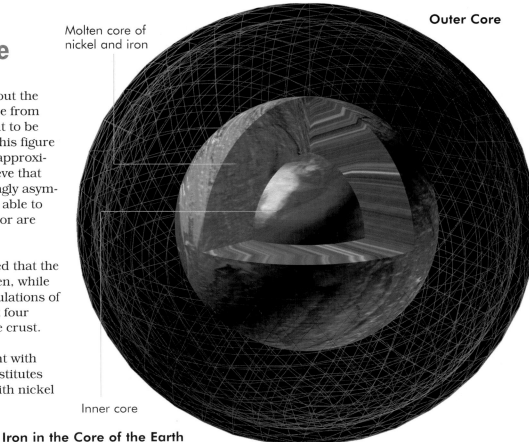

Outer Core

Inner core

Iron in the Core of the Earth

This theory has met with general acceptance, as investigations have found that meteorites (debris from other heavenly bodies) have the same composition.

According to another theory, the heat set free by solidification of the inner iron core leads to faster convection currents (compared with the mantle) in the outer core, which influence or cause the earth's magnetic field.

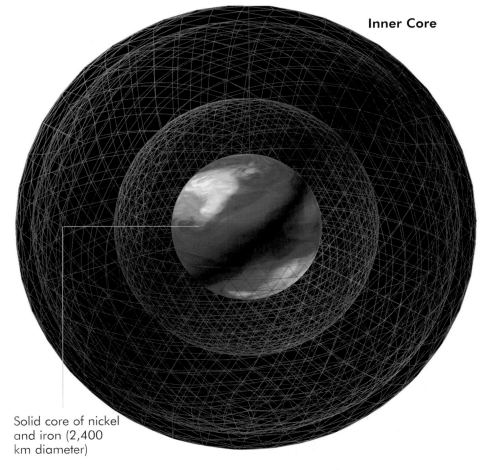

Inner Core

Solid core of nickel and iron (2,400 km diameter)

11

Earthquakes

"The sea swelled up in the harbour with spray and foam, and the ships at anchor broke into pieces. The streets and squares were filled with whirlwinds of flame and ash; the houses collapsed, the roofs fell through to the ground and the foundations were torn apart. Thirty thousand people of all ages and both sexes were buried under the rubble and crushed." (Voltaire: "Candide").

In these words Voltaire described the earthquake of 1755 that destroyed Lisbon and claimed 30,000 human lives. Many contemporaries saw the catastrophe as a just punishment for their sinful way of life. Every year more than a million earthquakes take place on the earth. However, most of them are so weak as to be completely unnoticeable to humans.

According to the geographical location of the source, we distinguish between earthquakes and seaquakes. The distinctions between local quakes, close quakes, distant quakes and far distant quakes correspond to the distance from the source. In a local quake the observation post is inside the quaking area, in close quakes less than 1,000 km from the source, in distant quakes up to 10,000 km or even further from the source.

According to their strength quakes are classified as small, medium, large or global quakes. The most powerful quakes are recorded all over the world. According to the depth of the source we distinguish between earthquakes close to the surface, normal quakes and deep quakes.

From the source of the earthquake, concentric oscillations travel across the whole earth. They are called seismic waves. "Seismos" is a Greek work meaning "shaking". The most powerful ground motion takes place close to the so-called epicentre. The movements are analysed with instruments and by observation of the terrain. The most important instrument for measuring and investigating earthquakes is the seismograph. It records the waves produced by the quake. In order to gain precise recordings, the seismograph must have as little contact with the ground as possible, so that constant motions of the earth can be ignored. For this reason efforts are made to disconnect seismographs from subterranean movements by means of special attachments with springs or hinges.

Distances from the source of an earthquake can be established with the help of a seismic time curve. The basis for this is the arrival of various types of wave at specified observation posts at different times. From this data it is possible to calculate the distance to the epicentre. Today this is carried out by means of up-to-date computer technology.

After an earthquake has been located, its strength as measured in magnitudes is expressed on the Richter scale. The Californian seismologist Charles Richter introduced the classification of the strength of earthquakes in 1935. A measurement of intensity taken from observed effects of the earthquake, and expressing its subjective strength, is made according to the Mercalli scale.

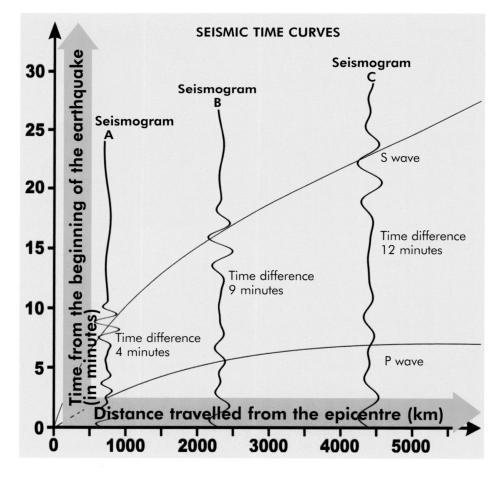

SEISMIC TIME CURVES

Seismogram A

Seismogram B

Seismogram C

S wave

Time difference 12 minutes

Time difference 9 minutes

Time difference 4 minutes

P wave

Time from the beginning of the earthquake (in minutes)

Distance travelled from the epicentre (km)

Causes/Origin

In the time of the Greek philosopher Aristotle, it was believed that earthquakes were caused by subterranean fire and storms. In ancient Japan people believed that the movements of an enormous fish, which carried the earth, caused it to quake. Today we have a fairly exact idea of the causes. 90% of all earthquakes are directly connected with tectonic processes in the lithosphere. Most quakes arise along the boundaries of plates. These plates either slide along each other, collide or break apart.

When plates move away from each other, only small earthquakes arise. There are various causes of stronger shocks: when one plate pushes over another, enormous pressure is built up that can suddenly be released at some stage and lead to an earthquake, for example in Mexico City in 1985 (10,000 dead).

Horizontal displacement can be seen at the San Andreas fault, which runs along the boundary between the North American and Pacific plates. In the Loma Prieta earthquake in 1989 the North American plate rose by 1 m and the Pacific plate moved 2 m to the north-west. Fortunately most of the shock waves were absorbed below ground.

Movements along a vertical fault line, as for example in the earthquake of 1988 in Armenia, are the most common cause of quakes. In Armenia the source of the quake was 10 km below the ground, but the shock waves penetrated right to the surface.

Earthquakes that originate at depths of more than 100 km usually happen at the edges of continents or on chains of islands located close to deep sea trenches or young volcanic

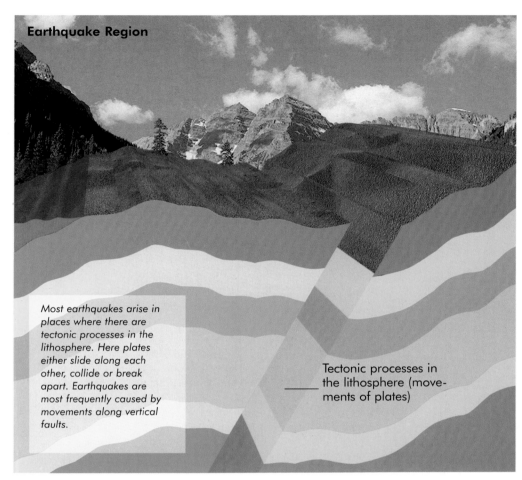

Earthquake Region

Most earthquakes arise in places where there are tectonic processes in the lithosphere. Here plates either slide along each other, collide or break apart. Earthquakes are most frequently caused by movements along vertical faults.

Tectonic processes in the lithosphere (movements of plates)

mountains, such as the Japanese islands and the west coast of South America. Here the plates collide, so that the surface forced downwards disappears beneath the upper plate into the mantle.

The sources of earthquakes are located on a plane sloping from the ocean to the land. They are at depths of up to 700 km. This area is known as the Wadati-Benioff zone. Horizontal movements can also take place in these areas, however. In 1995 parts of Port Island and Rokko Island were displaced by 4 m! A normal displacement is between 10 and 20 cm.

Regions further from the edges of tectonic plates suffer from large quakes much less often. Such regions include northern Europe and the east of the United States. Never-

theless a quake shook the city of London in 1750, and in 1811 there were several quakes in Missouri. There is still no clear explanation for these earthquakes in the middle of continental plates. It is possible that they are caused by unknown plate boundaries deep in the earth's crust.

7% of all earthquakes are of volcanic origin. These are so-called eruption quakes. In terms of timing, location and cause, their shock waves are connected with volcanic activity.

3% can be classified as quakes caused by collapse. This happens when the roof of a subterranean cavity collapses. There are a number of ways in which the cavity may have formed. The shock from the resulting central quake has only a short range.

Continental Drift

Pangaea

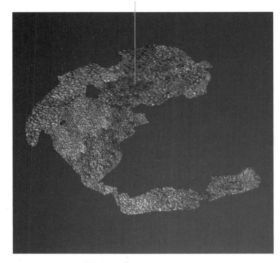

300 million years ago

When looking at a map of the world we notice straight away how well Africa and South America fit together. South Australia can easily be joined to the Antarctic, and so on.

Investigations showed that certain sorts of rock of the same type and age are to be found both in Brazil and in south-west Africa. The samples found are at least two billion years old. An identical

Gondwana   Laurasia

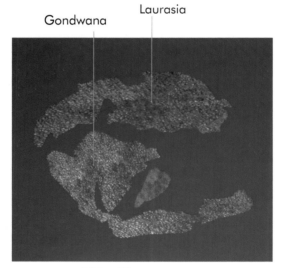

250 million years ago

sequence of glaciation, sedimentation, formation of coal etc, showed that these two continents were once joined. For example, a reptile fossil from the Permian period about 280 million years ago has been found only in South Africa and southern Brazil.

Rocks that can be formed only under certain climatic conditions are found in places where these conditions have never existed. Examples of this are coal deposits in the Antarctic and evidence that enormous masses of ice used to exist in South Africa.

From all of these findings we are forced to the conclusion that our continents are not fixed and immovable, but change their shape and position over time.

Alfred Wegener (1880–1930), constantly in search of proof for the theory of continental drift, provided decisive arguments with his book about the formation of continents and oceans, published in 1915.

According to his theory there must once have been a "supercontinent" containing the whole land

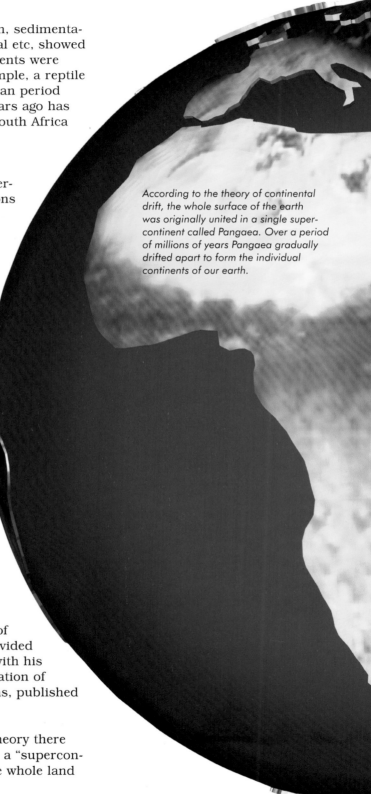

According to the theory of continental drift, the whole surface of the earth was originally united in a single supercontinent called Pangaea. Over a period of millions of years Pangaea gradually drifted apart to form the individual continents of our earth.

surface of the earth. He called this Pangaea (Greek, meaning "all the land"). At some stage it drifted apart to form several continents. About 250 million years ago Pangaea began to split into two large continents: Laurasia in the north and Gondwanaland in the south.

About 180 million years ago Gondwanaland was divided into three parts, giving rise to Australia-Antarctic, South America-Africa and India. The opening of the South Atlantic about 130 million years ago separated South America from Africa. India moved towards Asia, colliding with it about 45 million years ago. Australia and the Antarctic drifted apart about 45 million years ago. Laurasia split up into Europe, Asia and North America about 10 million years ago.

As already mentioned, the evidence for Wegener's theories consisted in the way the continents fit together, but also geological similarities such as the age of rocks and geological structures as well as the presence of the same fossils on both sides of the Atlantic. However, plausible explanations for the separation of Pangaea were not available.

Gondwana   Laurasia

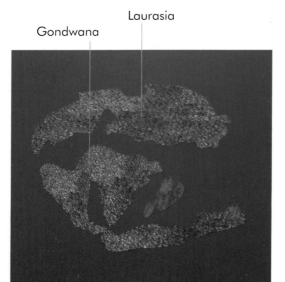

130 million years ago

Only in recent decades have Wegener's ideas been convincingly confirmed and further developed.

As a consequence of the discovery of the lithospheric plates, on which the continents move, the formation of new oceanic crust by sea-floor spreading, on the one hand, and the theory of continental drift, on the other hand, was expanded into the modern theory of plate tectonics.

Eurasia

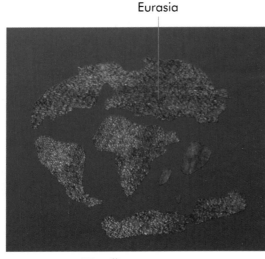

45 million years ago

15

Plate Tectonics

Movement of Plates   An uncertain process

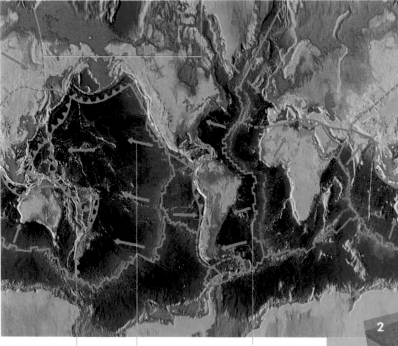

Subducting plate boundary   Direction of movement of plate   Constructive plate boundary

Direction of plate movement

Convection currents inside the earth

Plates slide along one another

Cooler material sinks

Hot materials flows upwards

Chain of volcanic islands from hot spot

Convection currents inside the earth

Source of magma beneath earth's crust

Direction of plate movement

Convection currents inside the earth

Mid-Atlantic ridge

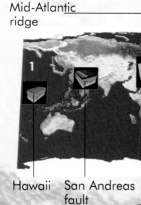

Hawaii   San Andreas fault

Inner core

Outer core

Although Alfred Wegener succeeded in providing convincing proof of continental drift, he searched in vain for the causes of these movements, which are today described using the term "plate tectonics" or "convection tectonics".

Today we know that the earth's crust, together with the uppermost part of the earth's mantle, the lithosphere, consists of a number of plates. These plates lie on top of the softer asthenosphere and form the base for continents and oceans. Seven large plates, such as the Pacific and Eurasian plates, have been identified. A large number of smaller plates have also been discovered, for example the Mediterranean and Near Eastern plates.

The thickness of the plates, which are continually moving, varies from 50 to 200 km. Larger plates have an area of 65 million km². The plates can make horizontal movements, in this way either moving away from neighbouring plates (divergent plate boundaries) or colliding with other plates (convergent plate boundaries). They can also simply slide past each other (transform boundaries). Here we speak of transform effects.

Current opinion holds that convection currents in the interior of the earth are responsible for all these movements.

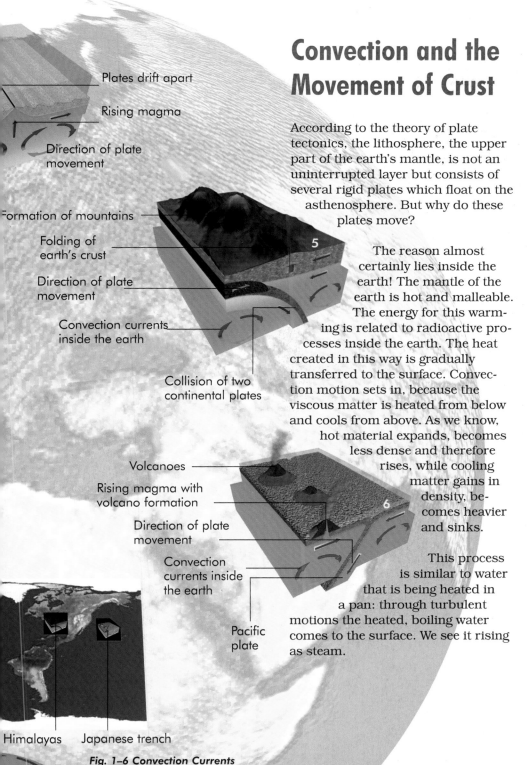

Plates drift apart

Rising magma

Direction of plate movement

Formation of mountains

Folding of earth's crust

Direction of plate movement

Convection currents inside the earth

Collision of two continental plates

Volcanoes

Rising magma with volcano formation

Direction of plate movement

Convection currents inside the earth

Pacific plate

Himalayas   Japanese trench

Fig. 1–6 Convection Currents
According to the theory of plate tectonics, the lithosphere consists of several large plates floating on the asthenosphere, the molten part of the earth's mantle. Their movements are caused by convection currents in the earth's mantle beneath the lithosphere. Convection motion arises in flowing matter when it is heated from below and its upper surface cools. Hot matter with a lower density rises, and cooler matter from the surface with its higher density sinks. At places where the hot matter rises and flows to the side in opposite directions, the plates slide past each other or are separated. At other plate boundaries the cold matter sinks into the earth and pulls the plates down with it.

Convection and the Movement of Crust

According to the theory of plate tectonics, the lithosphere, the upper part of the earth's mantle, is not an uninterrupted layer but consists of several rigid plates which float on the asthenosphere. But why do these plates move?

The reason almost certainly lies inside the earth! The mantle of the earth is hot and malleable. The energy for this warming is related to radioactive processes inside the earth. The heat created in this way is gradually transferred to the surface. Convection motion sets in, because the viscous matter is heated from below and cools from above. As we know, hot material expands, becomes less dense and therefore rises, while cooling matter gains in density, becomes heavier and sinks.

This process is similar to water that is being heated in a pan: through turbulent motions the heated, boiling water comes to the surface. We see it rising as steam.

The consequences of this for the movement of the earth's crust are as follows. Where hot material ascends from inside the earth and flows off sideways, the plates are pulled in opposite directions and separated from one another, as under the mid-ocean ridge. Hot magma rises there and spreads out sideways. In cooling it solidifies and forms the lithosphere. At other plate boundaries in the subduction zones, cold material sinks and draws the plates down with it. The sinking matter consists of cold lithosphere material.

These currents should not be thought of as fast flowing movements, but as a scarcely measurable process ranging between a few millimetres and several centimetres per year.

These currents undoubtedly flow at varying speeds at different times and places. Some geologists believe that convection currents take place only in the mantle. Others take the view that the currents go deep into the core of the earth. Although geologists do not agree on the details, they are unanimous in believing that convection from the interior to the surface, through which sea-floor spreading takes place, is an important process, by means of which the earth has cooled down in the course of its geological development to the present day.

The heat energy inside the earth, although only one five-thousandth of the energy of the sun, is sufficient for the movement of the plates and thus for the emergence of mountains and for earthquakes.

From investigations of volcanoes, seismic waves and laboratory work, geologists can estimate a temperature curve for the earth. According to their calculations, towards the centre of the earth the temperature rises to 4,000–5,000°C.

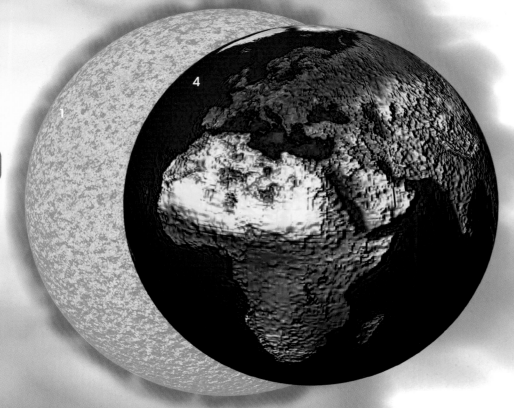

Fig. 1–4 Contraction Theory
Alongside the disproved theory that the earth expands and the crust bursts, the contraction theory gained acceptance for a long time. It said that the earth slowly contracted during the cooling process and its surface became smaller. As a result areas of the crust were pushed over each other, forming a high-relief surface with valleys and mountains.

Formation of Mountains

Since ancient times humankind has considered the question of the origin of mountains. Only in the last 150 years, however, have theories been put forward that can be taken seriously.

Supporters of the so-called contraction theory (Professor Eduard Suess, geologist, 1831–1914) held the opinion that the earth was originally a glowing molten ball. During the cooling process, they believed, it shrank and its surface became smaller. The solidified crust of the earth contracted, and surfaces were pushed over each other. Some parts collapsed.

Another group of geologists, including the English physicist Paul Dirac (1937), developed an expansion theory. Their assumption was that the earth was continually expanding, because gravity in the cosmos was becoming weaker and

weaker. At some period this caused the earth's crust to burst. By expanding more and more the earth became flatter, resulting in compression and folding, i. e. the formation of mountains. By means of this theory the formation of trenches could be explained, but not the alignment of mountain ranges or the differences in processes of mountain formation.

Only by modern-day findings of the plate-tectonic theory, these theories could be refuted. Today we know that the earth cannot contract, because new crust rock continually forms in the oceans by the outflow of molten magma from the earth's mantle to the surface. We also know that mountain ranges consist of layers of rock, lying one above the other, that are subject to a constant process of change.

Volcanoes

Volcanoes take their name from the Roman god of fire, Vulcan. The ancient Romans believed that a volcano near Naples was the entrance to the underworld. According to a Greek myth, the forge of the god Hephaistos lay below volcanoes. When the gods had an outburst of anger, humans were punished by the fire of an erupting volcano. In order to placate the gods, there were even human sacrifices in lakes of lava.

Volcanoes arise on the earth's surface, both on land and under the sea, through magma pushing up from the interior of the earth.

The lava hurled out during volcanic activity is transported from varying depths in the earth's crust through a chimney to the centre of the eruption, the crater. Depending on the way the lava is ejected, walls or cones form around the crater.

If we examine the distribution of volcanoes over the earth, we see that almost all of them are to be found in a belt of only a few hundred kilometres. By contrast there are few volcanoes in the interior of continents.

Most volcanoes are connected to the boundaries of the large plates of the earth's crust. They are located at the mid-ocean ridges, on chains of island and at several large continental rifts, in zones where continental plates collide with a subducted plate or inside the plate boundaries, for example the boundary of the Pacific plate.

Volcanic Eruption

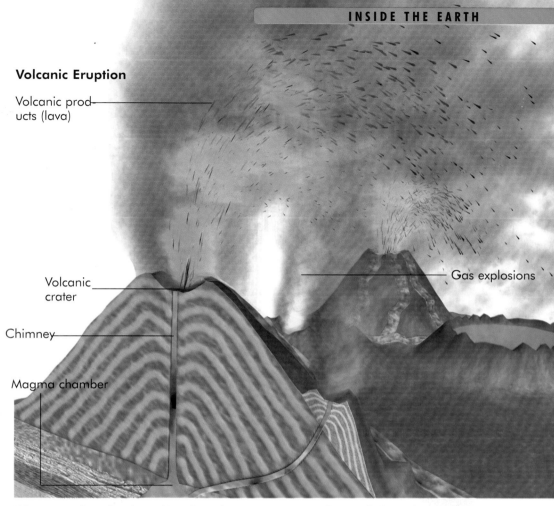

Volcanic products (lava)

Volcanic crater

Chimney

Magma chamber

Gas explosions

Volcanoes are formed on the earth's surface when magma presses up from inside the earth. Via a chimney the magma moves to a place of eruption known as a crater. The volcanic matter hurled out is called lava. The molten lava, often accompanied by showers of ash and gas explosions, streams downwards from the summit of the volcano cone and often destroys whole expanses of land.

Volcanoes are a serious danger to humans. Their lava flow can attain speeds of up to 50 km/h for long distances. They stream over enormous areas. In the case of volcanic eruptions along a deep sea ridge, lava consisting of basalt flows out slowly and fills the trenches created by plates drifting away from each other. Other areas of volcanic activity are characterised by hot springs such as geysers, solfataric fields, boiling mud pools and hot mineral springs. Showers of ash rain destroy vegetation, start fires and kill people. Compared with other disasters that occur every year, such as floods and earthquakes, or traffic accidents, the number of deaths from volcanic eruptions is relatively small.

Volcanoes also have beneficial effects for local inhabitants. On the slopes of Vesuvius, for example, particularly large and sweet grapes grow, leading to a flourishing wine trade. Showers of ash rich in nutrients (potassium and phosphate) improve the soil, so that it can be farmed after only a few years.

However, if thick layers of ash or streams of lava cover the earth, decades pass before the first lichens and mosses begin to turn it into fertile soil. Pumice stone, a light volcanic rock, is a raw material for industry. The cooling of molten volcanic matter in cavities gives rise to large crystals of agate and diamonds, for example, that can be polished to form precious stones.

Rocks

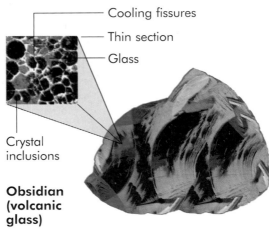

- Cooling fissures
- Thin section
- Glass
- Crystal inclusions

Obsidian (volcanic glass)

- Thin section

Granite

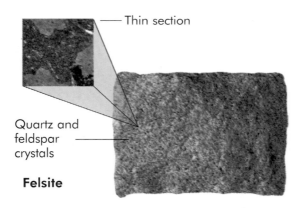

- Thin section
- Quartz and feldspar crystals

Felsite

Igneous rocks are created by heat and circulate inside the earth as magma. When it cools slowly in the earth's crust, the molten rock (magmatite) forms deep-lying rock and has a coarse-grained structure. Rock that flows out onto the surface of the earth cools quickly. The best-known, and one of the most commonly occurring, is basalt.

Rocks consist mainly of minerals. They are the most common compounds in the mineral world and are composed of only a few elements.

Most minerals are made up of at least two chemical elements. Only a few elements, such as gold or silver, occasionally occur in their pure form in the earth's crust.

A distinction is made between three types of rock: igneous rock, sedimentary rock and metamorphic rock.

Like the animal and vegetable worlds, the world of minerals is subject to permanent change. The surface of the earth is continually renewed by the circulation of rock. Igneous or volcanic rock rises to the surface, is eroded and becomes sedimentary rock. This is transformed into metamorphic rock and then becomes molten, later being converted into igneous rock. Sedimentary rock is the most common type of rock on the earth's surface. Beneath the surface igneous and metamorphic rock are predominant.

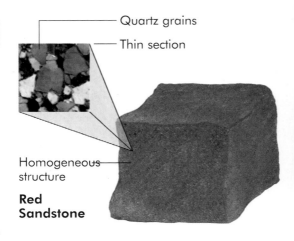

- Quartz grains
- Thin section
- Homogeneous structure

Red Sandstone

- Thin section

Sandstone

Sedimentary rocks include limestone, clay, slate or chalk. Sediments are deposits that become harder and harder through the pressure of the layers above until they finally turn into stone.

Increasing pressure

Shale

Phyllite

Schist

Chiastolite hornfels

Garnet hornfels

Migmatite

Increasing temperature and pressure

Metamorphic rock
Metamorphic rocks are rocks that have changed. Marble is an example of a sedimentary rock that has been changed into a metamorphic rock. Slate is transformed shale. It splits into smooth slabs. Gemstones are minerals that are used for jewelry.

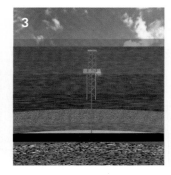
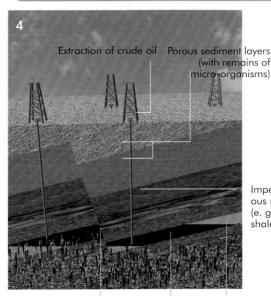

Extraction of crude oil *Porous sediment layers (with remains of micro-organisms)*

Impervious rock (e. g. shale)

Folding *Crude oil trap* *Natural gas*

Fig. 1–4 The Formation of Natural Gas and Crude Oil
In the Mesozoic, the middle period of the earth's history, large parts of Europe were covered with water, rich in micro-organisms but low in oxygen. As a result the process of decomposition of marine organisms that had died remained incomplete. The remains were concentrated on the seafloor, where they were transformed into organic sludge and bitumen below other layers of sediment. Through further flooding and the formation of land the pressure and temperature in the deeper layers increased, so that these substances were transformed into crude oil and gas. Sometimes gas and oil rise unassisted to the surface through porous rock. Usually they collect in so-called oil traps and can be extracted by drilling.

The Earth's Resources

Formation of Coal

Fig. 1–4
Our coal was formed over a period of many millions of years. At that time extensive areas of forest swamp covered the earth. Dead plants and fallen leaves sank to the floor of the swamp and under oxygen-free conditions ultimately formed peat. By a constant process of being covered by new layers, this peat was compressed and drained of water. As a result of pressure and weight as well as the heat that developed, the peat was transformed into lignite and with further pressure into coal.

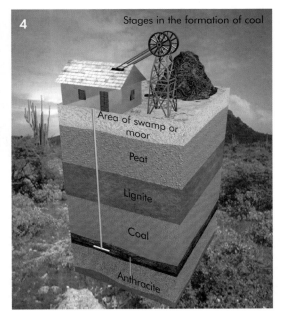

Stages in the formation of coal

Area of swamp or moor

Peat

Lignite

Coal

Anthracite

The earth's population needs increasing quantities of coal, gas and crude oil to maintain its standard of living. But how long will the reserves last? What will happen when they are exhausted? Where are these fuels found and what effects do they have on the environment?

Our present reserves are deposits that have already been discovered and are free to be exploited.

The total deposits of a raw material are described by the term "resources". Resources include known deposits that can be exploited today, those that can be exploited only at great cost or by new technologies, and deposits that have yet to be discovered.

Most resources are not renewable, because their formation takes many millions of years but they are used up in just a few hundred years. These include fossil fuels, such as crude oil, coal, gas etc, in particular. Salt deposits, ores and rocks are also important raw materials for humankind.

Since the beginning of the twentieth century, efforts have been made to develop alternative sources as substitutes, for example providing energy through the use of solar power or the development of industrial minerals.

The Surface of the Earth

The surface of our earth is the provisional result of diverse changes. The forces that shape the earth's surface can work on it from outside or from inside the earth.

External forces are the water in lakes, rivers and the sea, the wind and moving ice. The combination of all these forces leaves conspicuous marks and significant changes over the whole of the earth's surface.

Oceans and Seas

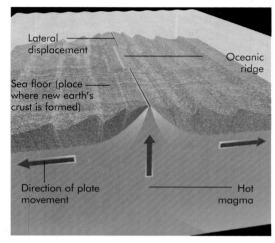

The sea floor is the place where new earth's crust is formed. At so-called oceanic ridges magma rises to the surface from inside the earth. The newly-formed, relatively light crust floats on the sea floor. If the crust reaches a mid-oceanic trench, it is pushed downwards by an adjacent tectonic plate.

The sea plays an important part in the geological changes to the surface of the earth. After all, 71% of the surface of the earth is covered by the sea. Yet the full dimensions of the oceans and seas remained almost unknown up to 150 years ago. Awareness of the effect of the tides and the power of the waves was confined to the coasts. Very little was known about the seafloor at greater depths.

Over a four-month period in 1872 a British naval expedition investigated the oceans of the world for the first time. During the expedition the first sighting of one of the longest and highest submarine mountain ranges, the so-called mid-Atlantic ridge, was made. Deep

plains, hilly areas, undersea volcanoes and a large number of trenches were also discovered. However, the fact that plate tectonic processes are a major factor shaping the variations of the sea floor was not appreciated until the 1960s.

Today numerous projects are devoted to how these structures were formed. Remote-controlled submarines are equipped to take samples of rock and sediment from the floor of the sea. Echo sounders transmit sonic waves to the sea floor. The waves are reflected, enabling the depth of the sea to be measured. Scanning by means of sonic waves makes it possible to create an exact profile of the surface of the sea. Other instruments investigate heat and magnetic properties.

Powerful surface currents, which influence continental climates, pass across all the world's oceans. Slower currents flowing in the depths of the sea are connected to them. The masses of water circulating in this way exchange nutrients,

energy and sediments. The motion of waves, variations in the sea level, erosion and weathering, as well as volcanoes and tectonic processes, have formed a varied "ocean landscape" in the course of the earth's history.

When we look at a profile of the sea floor, we see the variety of its forms. The floor of the Atlantic illustrates this: starting from the coast, the so-called continental shelf is located at a depth of 50 to 200 m. By moving across this surface for about 100 km we come to the edge of the shelf. Here a steep continental slope leads downwards. It is characterised by erosion channels, canyons and valleys. Its lower part is followed by the continental rise, which gives way to the deep oceanic plain after many hundreds of kilometres. Here sunken volcanoes, mostly extinct, are to be found. Some of these so-called deep-sea mountains rise above the surface of the sea as islands. Next to this zone the ocean profile gradually becomes steeper as far as the mid-Atlantic ridge.

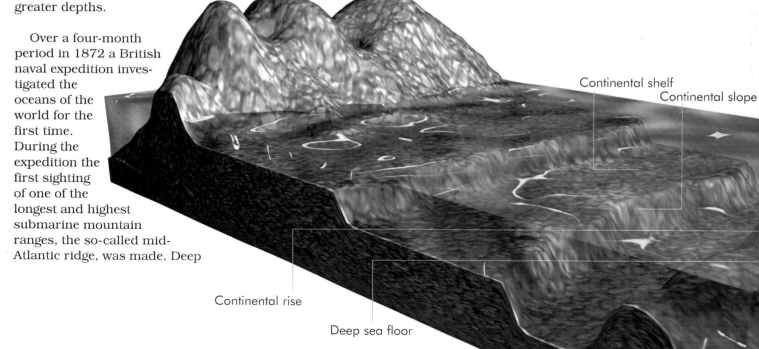

Continental shelf

Continental slope

Continental rise

Deep sea floor

Rivers

Rivers are among the most important geological forces affecting the surface of the earth. As they flow across a large part of the earth, they shape the landscape. Sediment is transported into the oceans by erosion. On their way to the sea, rivers form steep-sided gorges and coasts, create valleys and fertile alluvial plains. At places where the rock changes from hard to soft, rapids and waterfalls are created. If large quantities of sediment are deposited at the mouths of rivers close to the coast, a delta can be formed.

Rivers are important economic factors. As waterways they connect different countries and their industrial areas. A system of tributaries spreading out from a main river represents an important water reservoir for the population and industry.

Rivers are a decisive link in the hydrological cycle between precipitation and evaporation, between the atmosphere and the oceans. Most precipitation that falls on the land is carried back to the sea by rivers.

River Formation

The formation of a river begins with a spring, which often rises in high mountain regions with large quantities of precipitation. Initially the water flows to the valley in little rivulets. In this example, in glacial areas, it collects temporarily in a lake before gaining speed as a watercourse and continuing on its way until the river finally flows into a sea.

The Action of Rivers

With the scouring action of its flowing water, a river can create a deep channel. Loosened stones are carried along and deposited again in other places. This process is known as accumulation. The gradient and the volume of water determine how strongly accumulation takes place. The higher the speed of the current, the stronger the transporting power of the water.

A river transports its burden of sediment in three different ways. As so-called bed load the particles slide and roll along the river bed with occasional jumps known as saltation. As suspended load they circulate in the turbulence of flowing water and remain in a floating state. The dissolved load consists of dissolved materials deriving from the chemical erosion of rock and constituents of the atmosphere in rain water.

During transport pieces of rock are rounded by abrasion, ground into small pieces or also dissolved. After a distance of about 20 km, even hard quartzites have been rounded, so that in the lower reaches of a river there is no longer any bed load, but only suspended load and dissolved material.

In recent decades human intervention has had a decisive influence on the amount and type of material transported. The construction of dams has held back the suspended load and reduced the sediment burden. An increase in the river load takes place as a result of deforestation, ploughing or building work and the related erosion of soil.

In addition about 500 million tonnes of the products of human activity are carried into the oceans each year. This includes, among other materials, plastic waste, poisonous industrial waste, salts in solution and artificial fertiliser.

Lakes

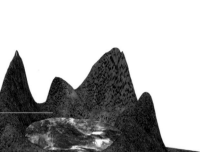

Formed when a river meander is cut off

Oxbow lake

A lake is defined as an accumulation of water in an enclosed depression or dip, normally over non-porous ground. Some large, land-locked lakes such as the Dead Sea are described as "inland seas" to distinguish them from the oceans and smaller lakes. The current in lakes is so small as to be almost unnoticeable. Smaller lakes, depending on their nature, are variously described as ponds, pools or marshes (shallow lakes).

With a total surface area of 2.5 million km², lakes account for 1.8% of the land surface of the earth. Lake Ladoga in Russia is the largest lake in Europe, while the Caspian Sea is the largest in the world.

The global distribution of lakes is highly uneven, and there are areas where they occur more often. Such areas are mainly regions where lakes were formed by the action of glaciers, especially in the Pleistocene period, for example in Scandinavia and North America.

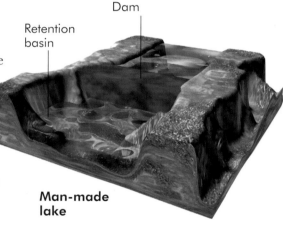

Glacier

Moraine

Mountain lake

Lake formation results from movements of the earth's crust

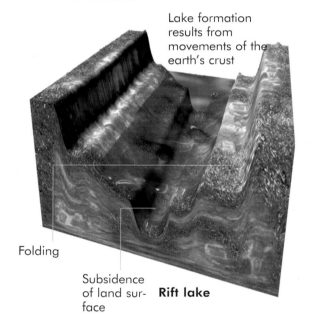

Folding

Subsidence of land surface

Rift lake

The water in lakes comes from the rivers flowing into them, from precipitation or from springs on the bed of the lake. We make a distinction between freshwater lakes and salt lakes. Salt lakes occur when the water cannot flow out. Drainage is therefore not possible, and the water evaporates gradually and the salt concentration increases. One of the lakes with the highest salt concentration on earth is the Dead Sea. It is approximately nine times as salty as the oceans.

Dam

Retention basin

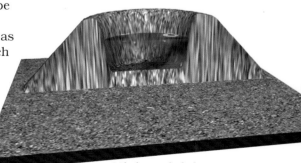

Man-made lake

Crater lake

Formation in an extinct volcano

Freshwater lakes are to be found where the water can flow in and out, for example as a lake behind a dam over which the water flows from time to time. Freshwater lakes are of vital importance to humankind, as they contain 95% of all the earth's fresh water reserves that could potentially be used as drinking water.

Mining pit lake

Coasts

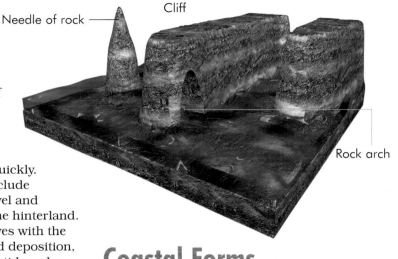

It is now customary to distinguish between primary and secondary coasts. Primary coasts, on which the action of the sea has not been strong, include rias, fjords, landslides and also tectonic and volcanic phenomena. Secondary coasts include coastal areas that have been subject to change in the form of depositions (spits of land) or growth (coral reefs, mangrove forests).

Coasts are highly changeable natural environments between the land and the sea. They constitute a significant area for humankind, as the coastlines have a length of half a million kilometres. Almost half of the world's population live within just a few kilometres of the coast.

Coasts change their appearance and boundaries relatively quickly. The reasons for this include variations in the sea level and geological changes in the hinterland. However, wind and waves with the consequent erosion and deposition, as well as currents and tides, also play a part in the formation of coasts.

In some particular cases humans can redirect the action of the sea on coasts, which is usually destructive, in order to gain land.

Coastal Forms

Different types of coast arise from the effect of the sea and from the tectonic structure as well as the composition and the movement of the land.

Cliffs – are caused by strong wave activity. Cliff coasts are often mountain coasts.

Flat coasts extend into the sea at a shallow angle, as with tidal flats, a coastal area that is flooded by the tides. Here the alternation of ebb and flow creates a unique natural environment.

Land spits occur where the direction of waves lies diagonally to the coast, forming a wall of sand. A river mouth keeps open a channel to the sea.

Fjord coasts exist in mountainous regions such as Norway, Scotland and Alaska.

Skerry coasts are formed on flat, rocky coasts with small, round outlying islands. There are many skerries on the south coast of Sweden on the Baltic Sea.

Ria coasts are formed by land subsidence. Examples of this are the coasts of Brittany and Ireland.

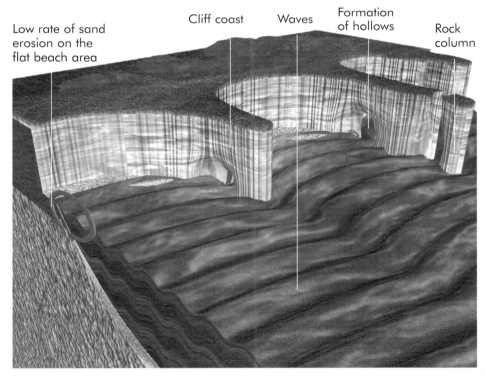

Coasts change through the action of wind and waves in varying intensity. When waves break on a flat section of beach, they gradually lose their force in the sand. The pull of the water takes little material back into the sea. When waves pound repeatedly on coastal cliffs, their force hollows out the cliff rock little by little. Sand and stones are loosened in this process and crash into the rock again with the next wave. In this way hollows and even arches can be formed.

Islands

Islands are areas of land completely surrounded by water. Islands close to the coast are usually remains of a land mass that was formerly connected. The causes of separation may be marine erosion (e.g. the Hallig islands in the German Bight), the breaking-up of adjacent areas of land (e.g. the Sunda Islands) or land

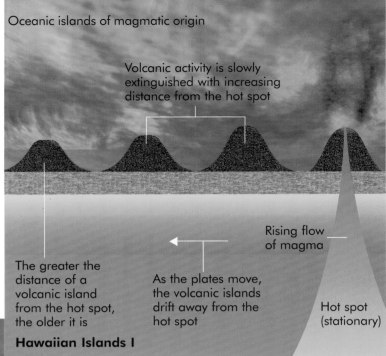

Oceanic islands of magmatic origin

Volcanic activity is slowly extinguished with increasing distance from the hot spot

Island formations such as Hawaii originate from so-called hot spots.

The greater the distance of a volcanic island from the hot spot, the older it is

As the plates move, the volcanic islands drift away from the hot spot

Rising flow of magma

Hot spot (stationary)

Hawaiian Islands I

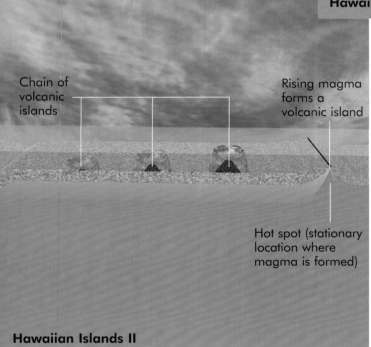

Chain of volcanic islands

Rising magma forms a volcanic island

Hot spot (stationary location where magma is formed)

Hawaiian Islands II

subsidence. The geological structure of the islands is similar to that of the mainland in such cases. The flora and fauna are also almost identical. Islands formed by deposition, such as some of the West Frisian islands, are constantly exposed to the effects of tides and coastal currents and therefore frequently change their outlines.

Some islands, for example Madagascar and Japan, were formed from parts of the continental crust that drifted away from larger land masses.

A special type of island is created when coral organisms colonise extinct volcanoes that formed on the seafloor. Most oceanic islands originated as magma. Some of them are volcanoes that have grown above the surface of the sea.

A large cluster consisting of a number of volcanic islands is formed in zones of sea-floor spreading. This is the location of the mid-ocean ridges, which in some place rise out of the sea as islands. This group includes Iceland and the Azores.

Volcano series (chains of islands) occur as a result of subduction processes. The islands of the Aleutian chain are an example of this. They were all formed at the same period of time.

Hawaii and the Canary Islands belong to the category of islands formed above hot spots. Here magma rises from the lower mantle of the earth and forms a volcanic island. If the oceanic plate moves on, further volcanic islands are created above the stationary hot spot. In this way a series of volcanoes is formed, in which the age of the individual volcanoes is greater, the further away they are from the hot spot. With increasing distance from the hot spots, the volcanic activity also lessens.

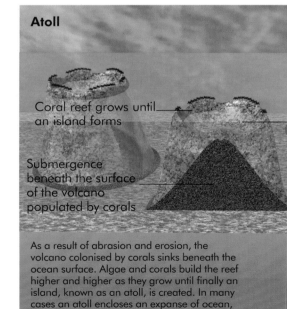

Atoll

Coral reef grows until an island forms

Submergence beneath the surface of the volcano populated by corals

As a result of abrasion and erosion, the volcano colonised by corals sinks beneath the ocean surface. Algae and corals build the reef higher and higher as they grow until finally an island, known as an atoll, is created. In many cases an atoll encloses an expanse of ocean, which is called a lagoon.

Atolls and Coral Reefs

Coral reefs or atolls represent a special kind of island in the sea. They occur in shallow seas, but also in the depths of the ocean.

In previous centuries researchers were fascinated by these "constructions". When Charles Darwin voyaged across the oceans between 1831 and 1836, he was one of the first to undertake geological investigations of coral reefs. The theory he then formulated remains valid today.

Corals are marine organisms that can only survive in salty water. Reef-building corals need relatively high temperatures of between 15 and 20 °C to construct their branching formations of limestone. They flourish best in tropical waters at maximum depths of 50 m. The eco-system of coral reefs includes lime algae, sea snails, crabs, sponges etc.

Corals often colonise the surface of underwater rises, especially volcanoes. Here they form circular reefs on the margins of extinct or dormant volcanoes. If tectonic processes lead to a fall in the level of the sea floor, or if post-glacial processes, i. e. the melting of glaciers, result in a rise in sea level, the effect is that a volcanic island sinks.

The upward growth of the corals produces an atoll. An enclosed part of the sea, the lagoon, is left in the middle of the atoll. It is surrounded by reefs. Lagoons can attain an area of 30 km². The atolls of the Pacific are long chains of islands that must have arisen from subsidence of the sea floor over a large area.

As a result, a fringing reef has evolved into a barrier reef, and as the island on which the reef formed submerged completely, an atoll was created. Other types of reef are formed directly along tropical coasts.

These are fringing or barrier reefs.

Fringing reefs are only a few metres away from the coast and often grow on rocks. If there is a lagoon – an expanse of water cut off from the sea – between the coast and the reef, the reef is known as a barrier reef.

The largest known barrier reef is the Australian Great Barrier Reef. It runs along the Australian coast for a length of 1,600 km, at a distance of 30–250 km from the coast. It is interrupted in only a few places by rivers flowing into the sea. They carry fresh water, which causes the corals to die in these places.

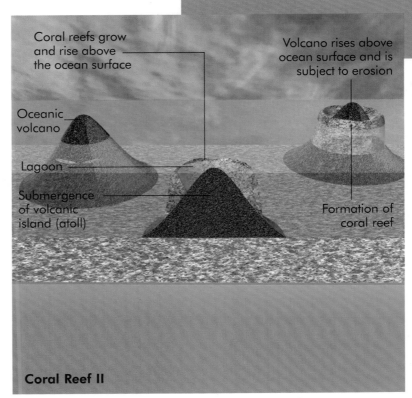

Coral Reef I

Formation of coral reef

Colonisation by algae and corals

Volcano risen from sea floor

Coral reefs grow and rise above the ocean surface

Volcano rises above ocean surface and is subject to erosion

Oceanic volcano

Lagoon

Submergence of volcanic island (atoll)

Formation of coral reef

Coral Reef II

Lagoon

A coral reef is formed on a volcano rising from the sea floor. The volcano grows to reach the ocean surface, then becomes extinct. Algae and corals colonise its coast and form coral reefs, which continue to grow in height on the margins of the volcano.

Deserts

Although, as far as human needs are concerned, deserts are hostile to life, their bizarre rock shapes, sand dunes and unique flora and fauna are fascinating.

As the only sounds that can be heard come from the wind, deserts are among the quietest places on earth.

There are deserts on every continent. They all have low precipitation, usually less than 25 mm per year. In the warmest desert regions of the earth, situated between 30° latitude north and 30° south, the air pressure is constant. The intensity of the sun's rays causes the warm air to rise. At altitude the air cools and the water vapour that it carries condenses, but no rain falls. The Sahara and Kalahari deserts in Africa are examples of this.

Deserts occur in more temperate latitudes too, as shown by the deserts of Central Asia and the Mojave desert in the west of the United States. These areas are either screened from moist winds by a range of high mountains, or the distance from the ocean is so great that the air has already parted with its moisture before it reaches the interior of the continent. In polar regions deserts are formed because the cold air can absorb only extremely small quantities of moisture, or the ground cannot retain the water, as on Iceland, for example.

The origin of deserts lies fundamentally in plate tectonic processes. The collision of oceanic and continental plates gives rise to mountain ranges, which cause a rain shadow. Other deserts came into being

Mushroom Rocks
Arrow = direction of wind

So-called mushroom rocks are created when coarse, heavy grains of rock are lifted by the wind to a height of no more than one metre. Only the lower part of the rock is worn away. Lighter, finer sand, which is blown to greater heights, erodes the rock less.

Deserts are landscapes with higher levels of evaporation than precipitation.

Dune Formations: Longitudinal Dunes
Arrow = direction of wind

Longitudinal dunes arise when the wind blows predominantly from one direction.

Dune Formations: Crescent Dunes
Arrow = direction of wind

Crescent dunes are formed in deserts where the wind blows constantly from one direction. Here the deposition of sand carried by the wind creates a concave curvature on the side sheltered from the wind.

Dune formations: Linear Dunes
Arrow = direction of wind

Linear dunes can stretch for many kilometres. They are formed when the wind direction remains constant.

Winds from land masses that are dry and at the same time warm play an important role in deserts.

Dune Formations: Pyramidal Dunes
Arrow = direction of wind

When the direction of the wind changes often, pyramidal dunes are formed.

through continental drift from high latitudes to low latitudes. Australia is an example of this. Its interior was once situated in a region of high precipitation. As a result of its northward shift into an arid, i. e. a dry, subtropical zone, the interior of Australia changed into desert.

The wind is the decisive force changing the surface of deserts. Its effects can be seen in the varied ways in which the sand masses are blown into dunes.

The shape of dunes depends on the amount of sand available as well as on the direction, strength and duration of the wind. Crescent dunes, or barchans, occur singly or in groups. They are formed when the amount of sand is limited and the wind always blows from the same direction. The ends of the dunes create a concave curve on the side sheltered from the wind. When a number of crescent dunes join up, linear dunes (transverse dunes) are created with long waving ridges at right angles to the direction of the wind.

Seif dunes, a type of longitudinal dune, are formed when the wind regularly blows from two directions. While the wind from one direction collects sand, the wind from the other direction blows the sand away at right angles to the first direction. If the wind is strong and enough sand is available, extensive sand seas, known as ergs, arise. They can cover areas of up to 500,000 km². An example of the effects of these forces is the great Arabian desert Rub el-Khali.

Star dunes or complex dunes are very high dunes with a height of up to 400 m. They are extensive dune formations like hills, consisting of dunes lying one on top of another. They move much more slowly than other dune types, sometimes only

50 cm per year. Other desert structures are pyramidal dunes and the fascinating mushroom rocks.

Water too plays its part in shaping the desert. Although precipitation seldom takes place, when rain does fall it takes the form of heavy showers that beat on the rock and encrusted earth. It scours deep fissures in the dried ground. Here the water collects in great channels known as wadis and carries large quantities of rock along with it.

Temperatures in the desert vary according to the location. Coastal deserts are subject to lower temperature fluctuations, on both a yearly and daily basis.

In deserts far from the coast the temperature rises as high as 50 °C in the shade in the summer months. In the clear nights the temperature often falls rapidly by 20 °C. In winter there are even frosts in high-altitude deserts.

Desert margins and semi-deserts are strongly threatened by the influence of erosion. Here, the levelling of terrain through the movements of water, ice and wind is closely connected to the process of weathering (erosion). One outstanding effect of erosion occurs during sandstorms in desert regions, when angular grains of sand are blown by the wind against hard rock surfaces, which then gradually look as if they have been worn away. This process is called wind abrasion. The grains of sand are themselves ground down and slowly rounded off.

Sandstorms are therefore a major threat for semi-deserts where the land is still farmed. In the dry season, dried-out arable earth (loose material such as soil and sand) can be carried away overnight by the wind, thus contributing to the spread of the desert.

Glaciers

Glaciers are bodies of ice created from the transformation of snow. 98% of the earth's glaciers are situated in the polar regions, the rest in high mountains. If these masses of ice melted, the sea level would rise by more than 60 m.

Phenomena caused by glaciers are described with the word "glacial". Glaciers are an important factor in shaping the landscape. They move downwards as streams of ice and produce deep valleys. When they melt in warmer regions, they scour out enormous quantities

of sediment load and deposit it again in characteristic formations.

During the most recent ice ages of the Pleistocene epoch, large areas of North America and Europe were covered with layers of ice similar to those in Greenland and the Antarctic today. Glacier ice can be formed only when the temperature lies below 0 °C and enough snow falls.

Freshly fallen snow consists of large, porous flakes that are light and full of air. The pressure exerted by snow falling later squeezes the air out of the flakes, and breaks down the crystal structure. The mass becomes denser and solid grains of ice called firn are formed. As the firn melts and freezes again, the remaining loose snow is also transformed into ice, creating a mass of pure grains of ice held together by ice particles. This mass is known as firn ice. Through its own weight and new snow the firn ice is compressed more and more until it

becomes a homogeneous glacier. Thin layers of glacier ice shine blue-green, while in reflected light the ice is white.

When the accumulated expanse of ice has become thick enough, it starts to move down the slope under the influence of gravity. The thicker the ice and the steeper the slope, the higher the speed at which the glacier moves. Alpine glaciers move at about 30 to 150 mm per year. Glaciers in the Himalayas move at up to 1,000 m per year, while those in western Greenland can even advance 7,000 m per year. Glaciers flow more quickly at the surface and in the middle than at the base and the sides. If a glacier flows through a crooked valley, the speed of flow behaves just as it would in a river, i. e. it is higher at the outside of the bend.

Glaciers move by gliding and by a process known as plastic flow. In warmer areas the process of gliding dominates. The outer margins of the glacier melt, and the meltwater flows off above and below the ice. These layers of meltwater act as a surface on which the glacier glides. In very cold regions this process of gliding does not take place. Here the base of the glacier is

Source of glacier with firn ice or glacier ice

Formation of crevasses due to varying rates of flow

Medial moraine

Lateral moraines

Snout of glacier

Glacial gate

Glacial lake

Terminal moraine

A glacier is formed when more snow falls than can melt during the course of a year. In addition to newly fallen snow, masses breaking away from the slopes (avalanches) provide further quantities of snow. After being compressed to layers of ice, it starts to move under the influence of gravity. As it moves, the ice picks up and crushes rock material in its path. These sediments are called moraines. They are deposited at the side as lateral moraines and at the end of the glacier as semi-circular terminal moraines. Glacier lakes often form behind terminal moraines, which can be very high.

frozen to the underlying rock. The boundaries of the ice grains and the crystal structure in the ice move a few millionths of a millimetre within the ice. Under enormous pressure the addition of these units of movement leads to the motion of the whole mass of ice. This is plastic flow. Crevasses, fissures in the glacier, occur most often where the ice is forced against a wall of rock and in the curves of a glacier valley. The downward movement of the glacier takes it into zones where the temperature is above freezing point. Here the ice starts to melt. On the way to this point the glacier ice has carried along an enormous mass of rock, the moraines.

A moraine is rock that has been transported and deposited by the ice. This rock can consist of pointed pieces but also of rounded stones that have been shaped by the action of the ice. We distinguish between different kinds of moraine. Ground moraines on the underside of a glacier derive from rock broken off or frozen off from the underlying surface, but also from the surface of the glacier, as loose material falls through crevasses to the base of the glacier. Lateral moraines store the material falling onto the sides of the glacier and carry it downwards, by which means walls are built up along the glacier. Medial moraines are created when two glaciers merge

into one. The lateral moraines at the inner margins of the two glaciers join to form a medial moraine, which then flows on downwards as a wall of debris inside the merged glacier. Terminal moraines are formed at the end of glaciers. They create a semi-circle around the snout of the glacier. These moraines can only develop if the end of the glacier remains in the same location for a longer period of time.

When a glacier melts altogether, it leaves behind a completely altered landscape. Cirques (bowl-shaped hollows) and ridges of rock have been formed by the constant erosion processes of carving out and scouring. U-shaped valleys have been created and fjords have arisen where they meet the ocean.

The Atmosphere

The atmosphere consists of about 78% nitrogen, about 21% oxygen, about 0.9% argon and about 0.04% carbon dioxide. Traces of neon, hydrogen, helium, ozone, methane and nitrogen oxides are also present. This surrounding layer has undergone many changes in the course of the earth's history.

When the earth was young, more than 4.5 billion years ago, the atmosphere consisted mainly of hydrogen, carbon dioxide and carbon monoxide. After the solar wind had blown this atmosphere away, gases emanating from the earth's interior built up a new layer. Its main constituents were carbon dioxide, nitrogen oxides, sulphur dioxide and water vapour. The condensed water vapour eventually became the basis of our oceans and seas, in which the earliest organisms developed. Two billion years ago they acquired the ability to photosynthesise and began to produce oxygen. This was the prerequisite for organisms that were able to breathe in our atmosphere for the first time, 1.5 billion years later.

Structure of the Atmosphere

The invisible layer of air called the atmosphere (Greek: ball of vapour) surrounds the earth like an outsized shield. Without it the processes of life on our planet would be unimaginable.

It is held in place by the gravitational attraction of the earth's mass, and rotates with the earth. The atmosphere, four fifths of which consists of nitrogen and one fifth of oxygen (with very small amounts of other gases), attains a height of 1,000 km and is divided into different "storeys", the spheres. The troposphere, stratosphere and ionosphere belong to the inner atmosphere, the exosphere to the outer atmosphere.

Three quarters of the mass of the atmosphere and almost all of its moisture is located in the troposphere, a belt 10 km deep. The troposphere is the area immediately above the earth's surface. The phenomena that affect our weather develop here.

The air is thoroughly mixed as a result of horizontal and vertical currents. With increasing altitude, the temperature falls at an even rate. Above the equator temperatures fall to –60 °C, above the poles to –50 °C in summer and –80 °C in winter. The most important weather phenomena occur in the lowest reaches of the troposphere, which is called the peplosphere.

Next to it is the stratosphere (Greek: layer), which extends to an altitude of up to 50 km. Between the troposphere and the stratosphere there is a layer several kilometres thick that permits horizontal exchange between the two spheres. This exchange takes place by means of powerful currents, jetstreams, with speeds of up to 400 km/h. The lower part of the stratosphere contains a layer that has great importance for us: the ozonosphere, which reduces the ultraviolet components of sunlight to a level acceptable to humans. In the stratosphere the temperature remains constant at about –50 °C, rises again in the ozone layer due to the absorption of ultraviolet rays, and falls at the upper boundary to the mesosphere to levels as low as –100 °C.

In the stratosphere the sun's rays have the effect of breaking down chemical compounds and releasing oxygen. This is thought to be one reason for the content of oxygen in the troposphere. Vertical currents ensure that the mixture of gases is uniform.

The next layer, the ionosphere, takes its name from the electrically charged molecules of gas present there. The ionosphere can no longer be described as air in the usual sense of the word. Here the temperature rises constantly with increasing height, reaching almost 2,000 °C at a height of 450 km. This continual increase in temperature is the reason why the part of the ionosphere up to 450 km height is also known as the thermosphere.

At an altitude of about 450 km lies the beginning of the exosphere, where oxygen molecules become more and more rare. This layer is vital to our existence, as it protects us from cosmic rays. In the Van Allen belt the radiating particles of

Geo-stationary TV satellites at an altitude of 36,000

Exosphere (up to 1,000 km altitude)

Thermosphere (up to 450 km altitude)

Mesosphere (up to 80 km altitude)

Stratosphere (up to 50 km altitude)

Troposphere (up to 10 km altitude)

Earth

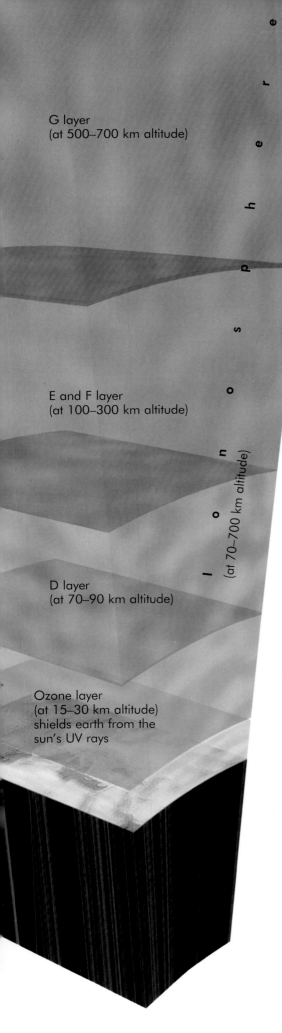

G layer
(at 500–700 km altitude)

E and F layer
(at 100–300 km altitude)

D layer
(at 70–90 km altitude)

Ozone layer
(at 15–30 km altitude)
shields earth from the
sun's UV rays

Ionosphere (at 70–700 km altitude)

solar wind are captured by the earth's magnetic field and prevented from reaching us.

The section of the atmosphere that is electrically conductive due to ionisation is called the ionosphere and is divided into the D, E, F and G layers. The D layer at a height of 70 to 90 km still contains almost all components of the atmosphere but has not yet become ionised and is not part of the ionosphere proper. From a height of about 100 km, where ionisation sets in, begins the ionosphere proper.

Two layers are situated at an altitude of about 100 to 300 km. The E layer, also known as the Heaviside layer, contains oxygen in atomic form that normally occurs only in molecular form as a dioxide (O_2). At certain wavelengths this layer acts as a reflector. This is the reason why long-wave and medium-wave radio can be heard beyond the transmitter's horizon.

The F layer extends to heights of about 300 km. It consists of ionised nitrogen. Above it at a height of 500 to 700 km is the G layer, which probably contains ionised particles from space. The ionosphere is thus the part of the atmosphere that conducts electromagnetic waves through ionisation.

High-altitude winds are a peculiarity of the atmosphere. After a weather balloon was launched in Hampshire, England in 1923, it was found four hours later in Leipzig, Germany. In this relatively short time it had travelled about 1,000 km at a height of 9,000 m, which corresponds to a speed of 250 km/h. This was the discovery of the jetstream, a strong current of air that can attain speeds of up to 400 km/h.

There are several systems of high-altitude winds, which can sometimes occur in lower layers of air but are normally found at altitudes of 9 to 15 km. The wind speed is usually more than 170 km/h. For this reason aircraft flying west avoid the jetstreams whenever possible.

There are two major systems of high-altitude winds. The circulation of winds above the subtropical regions of the earth is caused between 30° latitude north and 30° latitude south by convection currents of air warmed above the equator. They move parallel to a jetstream.

The other system of high-altitude winds is extremely complex and occurs in the middle latitudes of both hemispheres. The location of these winds changes constantly under the influence of areas of high and low pressure. These high-altitude winds are called circumpolar jetstreams.

The weight of one m³ of air is

1,200 g at ground level

500 g at a height of 5.5 km

1 g at a height of 48 km

Air Currents/Winds

Valley Wind Heated air on mountain slopes Air flowing into the valley Cool valley air

Mountain Wind Fast cooling on mountain slopes

Descending cool air, sometimes forms fog   Warm air in the valley bottom   Cold air descends

Systems of valley wind arise when mountain slopes exposed to the sun are warmed more quickly than the valley. As the warm air rises, the air pressure becomes lower than in the valley. This results in circulation of the air and produces a wind flowing into the valley.

In the mountains air cools faster on the slopes than in the valley bottom during the night. The cool air descends, so that fog often occurs at the valley bottom. At very steep mountain faces the air flows as wind to the valley exit.

Wind Systems

Earth   Area of low pressure

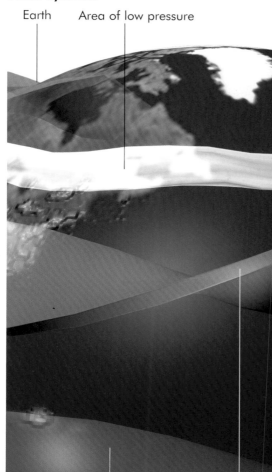

North-east trade winds

West winds

Weather on the earth is determined by the energy of the sun. Regions at the equator receive most warmth from the sun. Heated, moist masses of air swirl into the atmosphere. Here the air cools and water vapour condenses to drops, causing heavy downpours of rain in tropical regions.

But the tropical air masses also drift away to the north and south. When it reaches the troposphere the air is diverted towards the pole and descends again at around 30° of latitude. In this zone the air is exposed to higher pressure and loses its moisture. The dry, warm air creates the conditions that make land into desert. Some of the air descending from high altitudes returns to the equator as a north-east trade wind (in the southern hemisphere as a south-east trade wind).

This constant circulation between the equator and the thirtieth degree of latitude is called the Hadley cell. The name "trade wind" derives from

Wind systems are created by large horizontal or vertical movements of air. Here the temperature differences between the equator and the poles play an important part. They provide the energy for the atmospheric circulation. In addition factors such as cells of high and low pressure as well as the rotation of the earth determine the direction of the wind systems. The distribution of land and water surfaces also has an influence.

Foehn

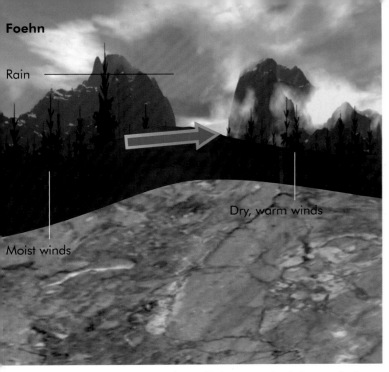

Rain

Dry, warm winds

Moist winds

When wind rises on a mountain, it cools. As this happens, clouds form and rain or snow falls. On the other side of the mountain, the wind, now dry, descends. It is compressed and warmed. In the Alps this wind is called a foehn, in parts of the Rocky Mountains chinook.

Offshore Wind

Rising, warm air over the sea

Circulation

Cooled air over the land

In the evening, air cools faster over land than over water, so that the air masses over the land descend and begin to circulate with the warmer air masses rising over the sea. This produces an offshore wind blowing from the land to the sea.

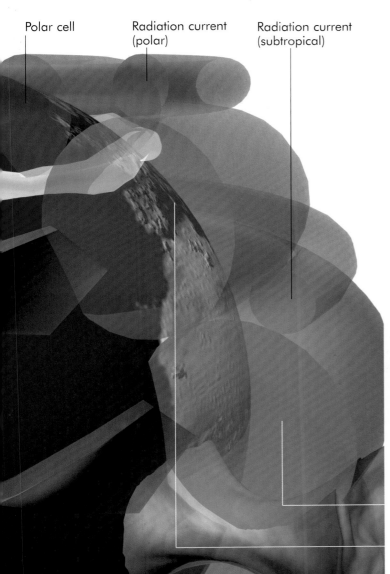

Polar cell

Radiation current (polar)

Radiation current (subtropical)

Hadley cell

Ferrel cell

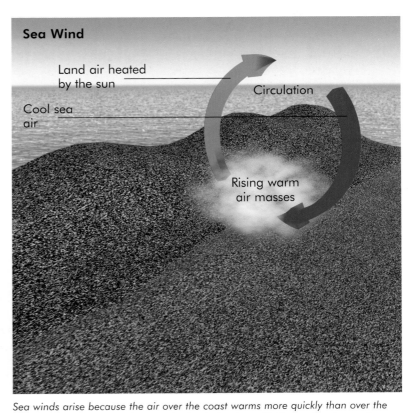

Sea Wind

Land air heated by the sun

Circulation

Cool sea air

Rising warm air masses

Sea winds arise because the air over the coast warms more quickly than over the water. Warm air masses rise over the land, circulate with the cooler air over the sea and push it towards the land.

39

the importance of this steady wind for navigating sailing ships.

Next to the trade wind zones is a relatively narrow area known as the horse latitudes, which are often free of wind. The horse latitudes change their position according to the time of the year.

Parts of the descending air masses flow north in the form of warm winds. In doing so they absorb moisture over the sea. At latitudes of 50 to 70° this warm, moist air collides with cold, dry polar air. Cells of low pressure responsible for the temperate climate of medium latitudes are formed at this polar front.

The Origin of Winds
Winds are caused by the pressure differences between neighbouring air masses. The denser air of a high-pressure area flows into the thinner and therefore lighter air of a low-pressure area. If the difference in pressure increases, the wind becomes stronger. When cold air meets warm air, a cold front is formed. The cold air pushes beneath the warm air and forces it upwards.

Belts of strong winds known as jetstreams can arise as a result of large horizontal differences in temperature and pressure. They have a dominant influence on the weather in higher mid-latitudes of the northern hemisphere. In the upper troposphere jetstreams attain a length of several thousand kilometres and a width of over 300 km.

The direction of the wind is defined as the direction from which the wind blows. The strength of the wind is given in km/h and on the twelve-point Beaufort scale.

In the lower layers of air, the strength of the wind is reduced by friction. Friction is caused by forests, mountains, buildings etc. Over open surfaces such as the ocean or desert, the wind force increases.

Wind alters the appearance of the earth. By gathering up sand or snow it removes material from the land surface. When they meet an obstacle, particles carried in the air at high speed have an effect like a sand-blaster. The force of the grains wears away rocks, for example. When the wind finally dies down, the material it bears is deposited. In this way the wind creates drifts of material.

By pulling at particles of water, the wind produces waves. If the wind exerts a constant force on a surface of water, a current arises, as for example the Gulf Stream.

Description	Wind Force	Km/h	Effect
Calm	0	0–1	Smoke rises vertically
Light air	1	2–5	Smoke rises almost vertically
Light breeze	2	6–11	Leaves rustle
Gentle breeze	3	12–19	Leaves and small twigs move constantly
Moderate wind	4	20–28	Small branches move
Fresh wind	5	29–38	Small trees in leaf begin to sway
Strong wind	6	39–49	Large branches move
Near gale	7	50–61	Whole trees shake
Gale	8	75–88	Twigs break off
Strong gale	9	75–88	Branches break off, roof tiles removed
Storm	10	89–102	Trees fall down, considerable damage
Violent storm	11	103–117	Trees uprooted, widespread damage
Hurricane	12	>118	Devastation to woods and houses

The strength of the wind is given on the twelve-point Beaufort scale.

Global Climate

Over the course of the year we see on the earth the same recurring pattern: circulating masses of air, and different regions with their different climates characterised by their typical weather phenomena. The most conspicuous feature of a particular climate is the vegetation.

The climate in general is strongly influenced by the characteristics of the earth's surface (altitude), the direction of prevailing winds and sea currents.

The global climate can change. 20,000 years ago, during the most recent ice age, the climatic zones shifted towards the equator and became narrower.

At present the general average temperature is slowly increasing, causing the climatic zones to shift towards the poles.

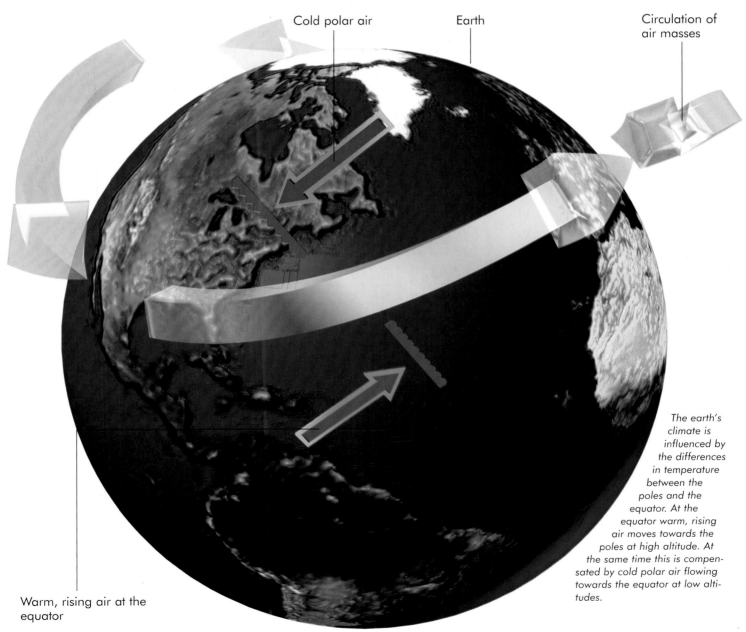

Cold polar air

Earth

Circulation of air masses

Warm, rising air at the equator

The earth's climate is influenced by the differences in temperature between the poles and the equator. At the equator warm, rising air moves towards the poles at high altitude. At the same time this is compensated by cold polar air flowing towards the equator at low altitudes.

41

Climatic Zones

Weather is the term for the state of the atmosphere at a particular moment. Observation of changing weather for a prolonged period gives rise to average measurements that permit classification into various climatic zones. Regions in the same climatic zone can be far distant from one another. The division into different climates makes it possible to describe and compare eco-systems and landscapes.

The high temperatures at the equator and the low temperatures at the poles are mainly a result of the angles at which the sun's rays fall on the earth. Nevertheless, regions with the same latitude do not automati-cally belong to the same climatic zones. Although the sun's rays shine at the same angle, other factors also play an important part.

Rapid warming in spring and rapid cooling in autumn take place only in the interior of a land mass. Coastal areas, by contrast, have different weather patterns due to a higher rate of evaporation. The average temperature is more even, as the water is capable of storing warmth. In addition cold or warm marine currents have an impact on the climate.

Climates are classified on the basis of temperature, precipitation and evaporation, as well as the way vegetation develops. Different types of climate can be described using the categories of the German clima-tologist Wladimir Köppen.

The wet tropical or monsoon climate is found along the equator. The average temperature is 26 °C. The climate is humid and charac-terised by lush vegetation and high, almost daily rainfall. There are no seasons of the year.

In South America and Africa the zone of savannah climate lies next to the monsoon zone. Vegetation consists of savannah forest and grass savannah. There is a rainy season and a dry season. Average temperatures are between 23 and 27 °C. The hottest time is before the start of the rainy season.

If the dry season becomes a season of drought, we speak of a steppe climate. This type of climate exists in North America in particular (prairie), and in Central Asia, North Africa and Australia. The vegetation consists mainly of grasses and shrubs, and there is more evapora-tion than precipitation.

In a desert climate the vegetation is even further reduced. Plants are to be found only in a few places. There is a very high fluctuation in temperature: 50 °C during the day and close to freezing point at night is not an uncommon occurrence. Desert climate is widespread in North Africa and in South and Central Asia.

Central Europe and parts of the USA lie in the temperate climatic zone. The summers are warm and dry, the winters cold and wet. Here a further distinction is made between a cold temperate climate and a constantly moist temperate climate. There can be precipitation at all times of the year, but extreme tem-peratures are an exceptional event.

Further north we come to the constantly moist snow-forest cli-mate. The average summer tempera-ture remains above 10 °C. The earth is covered in snow for months at a time.

In regions of tundra climate, where the temperature never climbs to 10 °C, only hardy plants can grow. Trees, for example, cannot survive in this climate. Even further north the frost is permanent. Precipitation is rare in the polar regions and falls as snow. Vegetation can no longer exist in these latitudes, where even the surface of the ground never thaws.

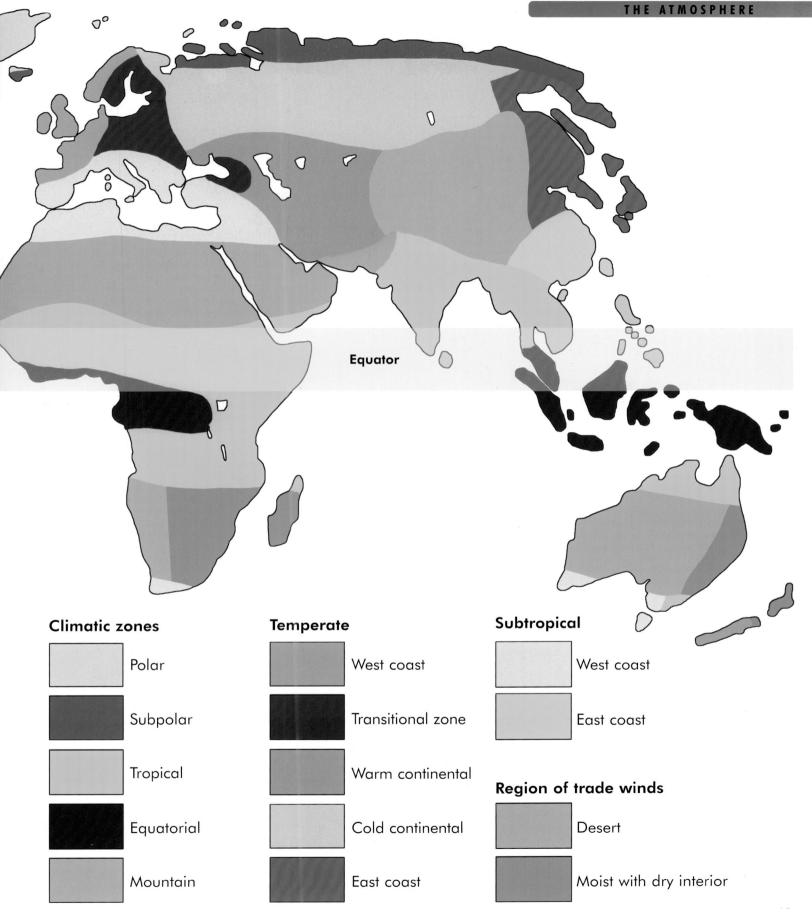

Equator

Climatic zones

Polar

Subpolar

Tropical

Equatorial

Mountain

Temperate

West coast

Transitional zone

Warm continental

Cold continental

East coast

Subtropical

West coast

East coast

Region of trade winds

Desert

Moist with dry interior

Formation of Clouds

Clouds are important in the circulation of water. Solar warming causes large amounts of water to evaporate each day over the oceans and continents. It rises into the atmosphere as water vapour. In this way more than 400 thousand billion tons of water are set in motion every year.

The shape and height of clouds are indicators of the air temperature and humidity. The movement of clouds shows the direction and speed of the wind. By correctly interpreting the clouds, it is often possible to make accurate weather forecasts.

A cloud consists of clusters of water drops and ice crystals. The diameter of the liquid drops is between 0.005 and 0.05 mm. When cooled strongly, they freeze. For clouds to form, water vapour has to condense. Moist air rises from the surface of the earth. This takes place in the case of rising air currents in the mountains, as a result of low pressure, or when the earth's surface is warmed by the rays of the sun.

Air rises when it has become warmer and lighter. At greater altitude the air pressure decreases and the rising air expands. In doing so it cools by about 0.6 °C for every 100 m. The colder the air becomes, the closer it gets to the temperature at which the water vapour in the air turns to water droplets, i. e. condensation takes place. This happens only if condensation nuclei, on which the water can gather, are present in the air. These are fine particles, either crystals of salt carried by the wind over the land or particles deriving from rock surfaces or gas emissions.

The main moisture-absorbing (hygroscopic) particles are salts, sulphuric acid and nitric acid. The number of condensation nuclei varies greatly from one region to another. Over the sea there are only a few hundred per cubic centimetre, but above industrial cities there are hundreds of thousands.

During condensation each of these particles is coated with a thin layer of water. Small droplets of

Thermic bubble

Rising air current

water are formed. Depending on whether there is a strong or weak vertical current of air, small cumulus clouds arise and, in combination with a strong horizontal air current, extensive areas of sheet cloud are formed.

Clouds are classified into a total of ten different types, divided into three "cloud storeys". They are situated in the troposphere, the part of the atmosphere in which meteorological phenomena mainly occur.

How Clouds Disperse
In the evening the earth's surface is less strongly warmed. The formation of thermic bubbles is reduced. The process of cloud formation comes to an end, and they gradually break up.

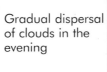
Gradual dispersal of clouds in the evening

Fig. 1 and 2, Cloud Formation
Clouds are formed from clusters of water droplets and ice crystals. When the surface of the earth heats up, the warmed, lighter air rises in a thermic bubble. In doing so it expands and cools. The colder the air, the more the water vapour condenses to form water droplets, which are driven out of the thermic bubble by the wind to form clouds.

45

Types of Cloud

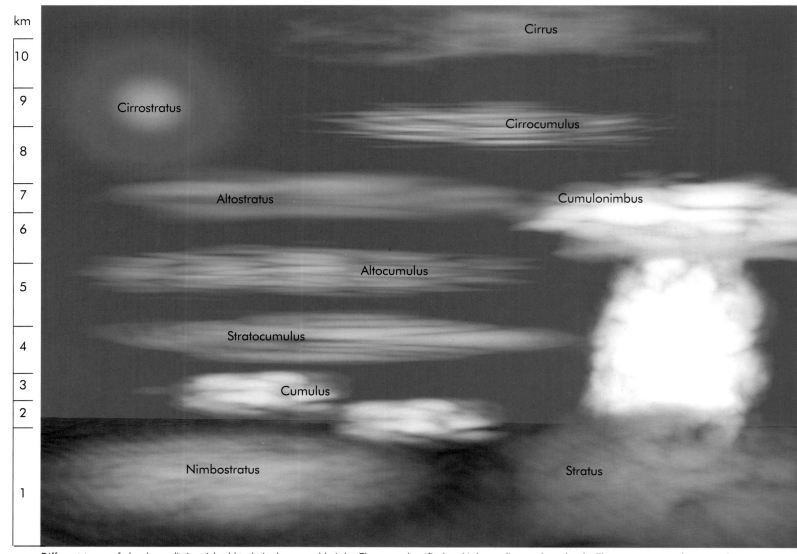

Different types of cloud are distinguished by their shape and height. They are classified as high, medium or low clouds. There are many sub-categories within these three cloud levels.

However varied clouds appear to be up in the sky, it is still possible to classify them according to their common features. In 1803 the amateur meteorologist Luke Howard (1772–1864) developed a table for distinguishing between different types of cloud and assigned Latin names to them. When classified according to their shape and height, the groups are as follows: high clouds, medium clouds and low clouds.

High clouds are grouped under the name cirrus. They include cirrus, cirrocumulus and cirrostratus. In mid-latitudes they are at heights between 5 and 13 km, in the tropics between 6 and 18 km and in polar regions between 3 and 8 km.

Medium clouds have the prefix "alto". They include altocumulus and altostratus. In mid-latitudes these clouds lie at 2 to 6 km, in the tropics at 2 to 8 km and in the polar regions at 2 to 4 km.

Low clouds are found at heights of up to 2 km. They include stratocumulus and stratus.

Clouds with a vertical structure can stretch across these categories of altitude. Their base is among the low clouds, and they are therefore allocated to this group. These clouds are cumulus, cumulonimbus and nimbostratus.

Cirrus

Cirrus clouds look like wisps of hair or feathers. They belong to the group of high-altitude clouds and are formed of ice crystals. At these heights (up to 18 km) they can attain speeds of 150 to 300 km/h. Sunlight can easily penetrate the thin layers of ice. At dawn and twilight cirrus clouds have intense, glowing colours. Cirrus are often a sign of bad weather.

Cirrocumulus

Cirrocumulus clouds sometimes appear in a wavy pattern and resemble the scales of a fish. They occur relatively seldom. With their rib-like appearance they join up like a number of balls to form a field of clouds. They are composed of ice crystals. They are formed from cirrus or cirrostratus clouds and are usually bad weather clouds.

Cirrostratus

Cirrostratus are high clouds like veils. They are composed mainly of ice crystals and form thin cloudy veils covering a large area. When these clouds pass across the sun or moon, they create a bright circle around them known as a halo. Cirrostratus clouds are often a sign of bad weather.

Cumulus

Cumulus clouds are detached heaps, looking like a cauliflower when they are large. The upper part shines a glowing white, while the lower part is often darker. They develop above all at midday and in the evening, particularly in summer. When they go on to form cumulonimbus clouds, heavy rainfall can result.

Cumulonimbus

Cumulonimbus are known as thunderclouds or clouds that produce showers. In the tropics they can grow to be 18 km high. A distinctive feature is a cap of ice at the top, which is a sign of thunder. Cumulonimbus clouds form on humid summer days. They often produce heavy precipitation such as showers of rain or hail, in many cases accompanied by stormy gusts of wind and thunder.

Stratus

Stratus clouds generally appear as a layer. They can extend from close to ground level up to heights of 2,000 m, and can be formed from rising fog. Their lower layers have no clear outline and look like plumes of fog. Stratus clouds consist of water droplets, or at low temperatures of ice crystals too. They are formed through warming of the ground. Stratus clouds can place a shroud of fog over mountains and tall buildings.

Nimbostratus

Nimbostratus are diffuse sheets of rain clouds. They are thick, grey layers that can rise to a height of 5 km. They are formed through the slow ascent of substantial layers of air, resulting in bad weather with long-lasting precipitation such as rain or snow.

Altocumulus

Altocumulus are coarse woolly clouds that look similar to cirrocumulus. They appear at altitudes between 3 and 4 km. When altocumulus clouds move across the sun, coloured rings of light arise, smaller than the halos produced by cirrostratus clouds. Sometimes individual patches of cloud are separated and move upwards. This special cloud type is known as altocumulus castellanus, and is a sure sign that thunder is approaching.

Altostratus

Altostratus are medium-high layers of grey cloud at an altitude of about 3 to 4 km covering a large part of the sky. These enormous clouds consists of water droplets and ice crystals. They are a sign of rain. If too much evaporation takes place, so that the rain does not reach the earth's surface, the underside of the clouds acquires a fibrous structure.

Stratocumulus

Stratocumulus are fine-weather clouds that occur at low levels. Grey or whitish clouds appear in heaps or as sheets lying next to each other or one above the other. No clear shapes or boundaries exist. Stratocumulus clouds occur frequently in the evening and in winter.

Precipitation

When large clouds rise, they soon reach altitudes where the temperature is below freezing. These clouds consist of ice crystals, water vapour and water drops that have not yet crystallised into ice despite the freezing temperatures.

The small ice crystals grow to be snowflakes that float to the earth's surface. A snowflake falls as dry snow on warm ground. If it passes through a layer of warmer air on its way to the ground, the snowflake melts and becomes rain.

The highest levels of precipitation in the world occur on Hawaii. In some regions here it rains 350 days a year. However, it is difficult to find out which place has the lowest level of precipitation, as there are several desert regions where not one drop of rain has reached the ground for years.

Rain

Most raindrops were initially snowflakes that melted as they fell to earth. The droplets or ice crystals that form in the clouds are too light at first to fall to the ground. Only when millions of these droplets collide, to form a drop, are they heavy enough to become precipitation.

Some flatter clouds produce only small drops that fall to earth as drizzle. When drizzle falls on frozen ground, it immediately turns to ice. All surfaces are then covered with a thin layer of ice, causing great dan-ger to drivers of cars, as this transparent ice is practically invisible on a dark road surface.

Clouds contain water vapour and cloud droplets, which are small drops of condensed water. For precipitation to happen, first tiny water droplets must condense on even tinier dust or smoke particles, which act as a nucleus. Water droplets may grow as a result of additional condensation of water vapour when the particles collide. Larger drops tend to be flattened and broken into smaller drops by rapid fall through the air.

Cumulonimbus cloud

Growth of drops accelerates due to opposite charge

Formation of droplets

Cumulus cloud

Stratus cloud

Droplets join together

Frozen area

Drizzle

Rain

Sleet

Dry snow

Formation of droplets and ice crystals

Ice crystal enlarged by formation of layers

Snowflakes

Wet snowflakes   Melted snowflakes

Snow

Snowflakes have a characteristic symmetry that reflects the way water molecules are fixed in the ice. However, snowflakes vary from this basic pattern. The reason for this is that the crystals grow at different speeds. No two snowflakes are identical. The individual snow crystals are so delicate that they break as they descend and collide. The crystals reach the ground as lumps joined together.

In the higher reaches of the clouds, water droplets and some ice crystals form. When the moisture from evaporating droplets is added, larger ice crystals are created. Finally the ice crystals join to form snowflakes. The flakes fall as dry snow on cold ground or as wet snow on warm ground.

Hail

The nucleus of a hailstone is either an ice crystal or a snow pellet covered in a thin layer of ice. In order for it to grow from a nucleus to a hailstone, new layers of ice have to be formed over and over again. Strong rising currents of air cause the hailstone to be repeatedly whirled upwards, capturing super-cooled water droplets as this happens.

The number of ice layers (up to 25) shows how often the hailstone was forced upwards in the cloud. The thickest layers of ice are formed while it falls, as the air humidity is higher at lower levels. When the air currents can no longer bear the weight of the hailstone, it falls to earth. This can cause severe devastation, as for example in the mid 1980s, when more than 200,000 cars were damaged in Munich during a shower of hail.

The largest-ever hailstone was found in South Dakota state in the USA. It had a diameter of 20 cm and weighed 875 g.

Fog

Fog is a layer of cloud at ground level. Extremely small drops of water are suspended in the air. This considerably reduces visibility. Fog therefore represents a danger for air, ship and road traffic.

Fog can also freeze. When mixed with exhaust gases and particles of dust it can become a poisonous smog.

Dew/Frost

Dew and frost are classified as precipitation, although in contrast to falling precipitation they condense on the surface of vegetation and other objects.

If the surface of the earth cools to below the dew point, dew is formed at temperatures above 0 °C and frost at temperatures below 0 °C. The dew point is the temperature at which the air is saturated with water vapour. When the humidity is 100%, the dew point is equal to air temperature.

Dew represents the transition from water vapour to water, while frost is the transition from water vapour to ice.

Dew and frost make up 3% of the total liquid amount of precipitation. As the quantity of precipitation varies greatly between the different regions of the earth, dew can be the only source of liquid for the hardy plants of areas low in rainfall.

Forces of Nature

There are many changes to the earth's surface that come from the interior of the earth. They include volcanic eruptions, earthquakes and the different kinds of movement resulting from plate tectonic processes. These can all have a destructive effect on the affected areas.

However, in addition to this, many threatening occurrences take place between the atmosphere surrounding the earth – with its clouds and layers of varying air pressure – and the surface of the earth. They include numerous storms such as hurricanes or tornadoes, but also monsoons. They are created as a result of the interaction between the evaporation of water from the seas and the circulation of air above them, as well as by the rays of the sun, which play a decisive role in these processes.

Thunderstorms pose just as great a threat to the earth, when lightning with a current of up to 40,000 amperes and temperatures of up to 30,000 °C tear through a channel of air. Apart from a few protective measures, we are as powerless against these forces of nature as against the catastrophes that come from the earth's interior.

Thunder and Lightning

Thunderstorms are an everyday occurrence. At any one moment lightning is striking somewhere on the earth.

The ground is warmed by the sun's rays. The rising warm air produces cumulus clouds, which can change into cumulonimbus clouds. High humidity levels, which we experience as sultry air, favour the formation of thunderclouds.

The upper parts of a thunder-cloud are mainly positively charged, the lower parts negatively charged. The reason for this is that the light, positively charged ice crystals are forced upwards by rising air currents, while heavy, negatively charged drops lose height. The lightning cancels out this difference in electric potential. By far the greatest number of strokes of lightning do not reach the earth, but are discharged within the clouds. If the lightning reaches the surface of the earth, then a so-called leader, which creates an electrically conductive channel, has occurred.

The lightning approaches the surface of the earth in steps from the negatively charged cloud. This lightning, called a stepped leader, does not hit the earth directly. A so-called upward streamer comes to meet it. As soon as the gap be-tween the stepped leader and the upward streamer has been closed, the lightning channel has been completed and the main discharge follows. It begins on the ground and leads up to the cloud. This is the stroke of lightning visible to us. It has an average length of 1,000 to 2,000 m. The strength of the current can be up to 40,000 amps.

Ball lightning is a special form of lightning that is well known but has hardly been researched. According

Lightning

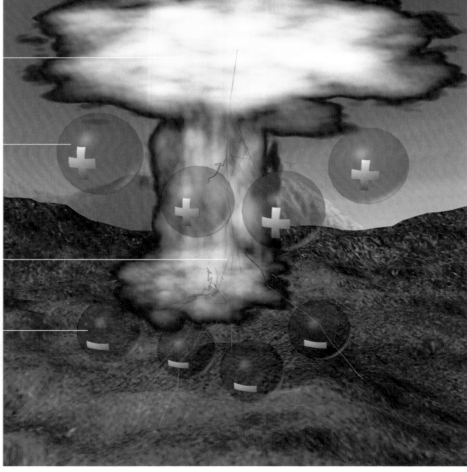

Thunder-cloud

Light nuclei with a positive charge

Lightning cancels out difference in potential

Heavy nuclei with negative charge

Differences in electric potential arise in a thundercloud when light, positively charged ice crystals are carried upwards by rising air currents and heavier, negatively charged nuclei fall. When the difference in potential has reached about 100 million volts, it is discharged by lightning within the cloud. This process can be observed in the form of so-called sheet lightning.

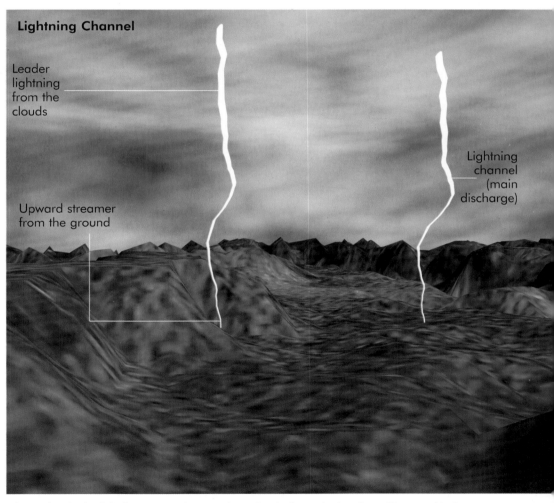

Thunderstorms
Formation of
cumulus clouds

Thunderstorms originate when the sun's rays strongly heat mountainsides, fields or other surfaces. During the day these surfaces heat up so much that eventually warmth and moist air rise, creating cumulus clouds.

Warm, moist air
rises

Thermic
bubble

destroyed whole towns. The lightning conductor, developed in the mid-eighteenth century by Benjamin Franklin, has largely removed this danger. The number of people killed by lightning has also been greatly reduced. The bodywork of a car is a metallic shield like a Faraday cage, and so provides good protection.

The potential danger therefore lies mainly in the electronics that surround us everywhere. Lightning can destroy computers or TV sets by penetrating to them through the electric wiring. Electronic aircraft components can also be destroyed by lightning, as happened in 1988 when an aircraft crashed over Germany.

Every year lightning causes several billion pounds worth of damage to electrical equipment.

to eye-witness reports, its size varies from that of a billiard ball to a medicine ball. It is thought to be a mixture of hot gases created when electromagnetic waves are emitted from the thundercloud after a lightning discharge.

We notice the lightning flash before the thunder because the speed of light is greater than the speed of sound.

The extremely high temperature of a flash of lightning (up to 30,000 °C) causes an explosive expansion of the air. This produces the bang that we call thunder. When the thunderstorm is further away, we perceive the thunder as a growling and rumbling sound. The cause of this is the reflection of sound by hills or high buildings or by the clouds.

Lightning remains a danger that should not be underestimated. In the past it often led to fires that

Lightning Channel

Leader
lightning
from the
clouds

Upward streamer
from the ground

Lightning
channel
(main
discharge)

When a thundercloud discharges onto the ground, an electrically conducting channel is created in the clouds. The lightning approaches the earth's surface in steps as a lightning leader. It is met by an upward streamer from the ground. When the positively charged stepped leader from the cloud joins up with the negatively charged upward streamer from the ground, a lightning channel is completed and the main discharge takes place. It begins as visible lightning on the ground and leads up to the cloud.

Monsoon

The Coriolis force, the deflecting force of the earth's rotation, diverts winds in the northern hemisphere to the right and winds in the southern hemisphere to the left. Monsoons are constant winds that change direction every six months. They appear mainly between 30° latitude north and 30° latitude south.

Their origin is to be found in the difference in warming between sea and land. The larger the land mass, the stronger the influence of the monsoon. The monsoon in its most highly developed form is encountered in South and South-East Asia.

When it is winter in the northern hemisphere, dry winds blow southwards from Central and North Asia. The air becomes warm over the Indian subcontinent and causes the months-long dry season.

In summer these winter winds give way to south winds. The summer monsoon blows over the sea. Through warming, humidity rises considerably. The enormous resulting increase of clouds leads to the well-known, long-lasting and heavy monsoon rains, which regularly cause flooding.

The largest amount of precipitation ever recorded within a month, almost 9,300 mm, fell in Cherrapunji in the Himalayas. This is over ten times more than the average rainfall for a whole year in Western Europe.

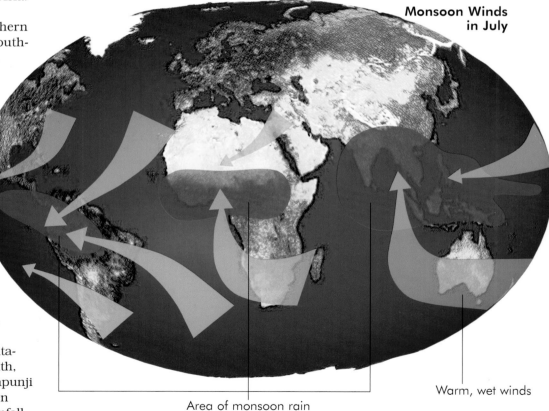

Monsoon Winds in January

Cold, dry winds

Area of monsoon rain

Monsoon winds change direction every six months. In winter cold, dry winds blow in a southerly direction from Africa and India. A cool, dry season results.

Monsoon Winds in July

Warm, wet winds

Area of monsoon rain

In summer, monsoon winds blow in the opposite direction. This means that warm air rises over the land. South-westerly winds carry moist air from the sea, producing heavy rainfall, especially in South-East Asia.

Tornadoes and Hurricanes

All those who complain about the low water temperatures on the beaches of northern and western Europe can console themselves with the fact that hurricanes cannot happen here. Hurricanes arise over tropical seas, where the temperature of the seawater is at least 27 °C. Regardless of whether these storms are called hurricanes as in America, cyclones as in India, or typhoons as in China, they bring immeasurable destructive power and terror to the coastal regions affected.

These devastating tropical storms always occur over warm seas and are marked by strong, spiralling high-speed winds.

Twisters, or tornadoes, are even faster and less predictable than hurricanes. They take the form of a funnel or tube, and consist of condensed water vapour. Their destructive power is limited to a relatively small area.

In addition to tropical hurricanes, spiralling storms that are much less charged with energy take place in mid-latitudes. These are the non-tropical cyclones, which last for a longer period and cover a greater area. They arise when cold polar air collides with a front of warm tropical air.

Hurricane

Spiral movement
of air masses

Hurricanes are caused by large differences in pressure between neighbouring masses of air. By means of a spiral movement of the air masses, a cold front and a warm front develop. Strongly rising currents of air cause heavy turbulence by cooling and thus creating condensation heat.

Spiralling funnel of wind (up to 500 km/h)

Tornadoes arise in thundery conditions when cold fronts break into warm air accompanied by strong winds at altitude. On the lower side of the thunderclouds a column-shaped rotating tube of air and water vapour is formed, extending down to ground level. At speeds of up to 500 km/h it races across country.

Hurricanes/Typhoons

Tropical storms are described as hurricanes only when they reach speeds of 120 km/h.

These storms have their own names in each of the tropical regions. In America they are known as hurricanes, in India as tropical cyclones and in China as typhoons.

The Australian Clement Wragge had the idea of giving names to hurricanes. He is said to have chosen the names of women whom he disliked. Since 1970 the first names given to newly-discovered hurricanes have been alternately male and female.

Hurricanes arise only over warm oceans, as a rule in summer or autumn. Enormous masses of cloud (cumulonimbus) are formed through evaporation. In-flowing wind creates a rotating movement around a cloud-free centre, the "eye of the storm". In the northern hemisphere the storm spins anti-clockwise, in the southern hemisphere clockwise. As no rotational impulse exists directly at the equator, hurricanes do not arise there, even though the water temperatures are high enough.

The rising air is whirled out-wards, while in the centre the air falls, is warmed and so loses its moisture. The "eye" of the hurricane becomes the axis around which the storm rotates and has a diameter of 15 to 50 km. The hurricane itself, by contrast, can cover areas as big as 1,000 km or more. Gusts of wind in such storms can reach speeds of more than 300 km/h.

When they race towards the land, they carry enormous masses of water with them.

Tornadoes

Tornadoes are mostly to be seen in mid-latitudes. They develop from thunderclouds and often occur in combination with hurricanes.

Tornadoes arise when cold, dry air overlays warm, moist winds. This produces heavy turbulence. Inflowing air currents cause a rotating motion, weak at first. The spiral contracts more and more as it develops, leading to a fall in pressure inside the column. For a short time this column, rotating faster and faster, can reach the surface of the earth. Nothing

can resist a wind moving across the earth on an unpredictable course at speeds of up to 500 km/h.

A tornado cuts a swathe across the country. It is only thanks to its short life, normally just a few minutes, and its small size, usually less than 100 m diameter, that whole areas of countryside are not destroyed.

The midwest of the USA is the area most severely affected by tornadoes, with 700 to 800 every year. In Europe tornadoes are a less frequent occurrence.

Houses are whirled about like building blocks, whole areas of land are flooded and subsequently gigantic mountains of cloud pour a deluge of rain onto the earth's surface. In the densely populated coastal regions of South-East Asia, hundreds and thousands of people are killed or lose their homes each year.

If the storms penetrate further inland, they die down relatively quickly, as there are no supplies of water vapour.

The formation of hurricanes is encouraged by the greenhouse effect. The areas of ocean reaching the dangerous 27 °C mark are becoming larger and larger. Besides this the oceans are warming up more quickly, which can result in storms beginning before the normal season in late summer.

Non-Tropical Cyclones

In contrast to tropical cyclones, also known as hurricanes or typhoons, spiralling storms with a much lower energy capacity take place in mid-latitudes: non-tropical cyclones.

These are immense areas of low pressure, moving in an easterly direction, which determine the weather for large areas of the earth over an extended period of time. They arise at a polar front, a boundary of air masses dividing warm tropical air from cold polar air. Along this boundary the masses of air exchange heat, in order to create an equilibrium in the atmosphere.

If the different masses of air collide, a warm and a cold front arise. The air masses move around each other in a spiral or in the form of a wave around the centre of the area of low pressure. Eventually the warm air rises and rides up above the cold air at the warm front. As this happens, clouds are formed, initially cirrus, later cirrostratus and altostratus clouds. Finally small amounts of precipitation fall from nimbostratus clouds. Only thin clouds are to be found in the wedge of warm air between the fronts.

In the occlusion stage that now follows (occlusion: from Latin for closing) the cold front catches up with the warm front, so that the remaining wedge of warm air is compressed and forced upwards. Cold air now occupies the whole area, and the warm air lies above it as an "inclusion". Clouds rise with it and the last precipitation falls. When all the air has ascended, the clouds disappear just like the fronts of the storm on the surface. This recurring cycle is a process lasting several days.

During this time the cyclones move with a so-called jetstream, which lies above them and carries them north-eastwards at a speed of 40 to 55 km/h along the polar front until they turn away towards the equator and so become slower, then finally dissipate altogether.

Non-tropical Cyclones

Cold air front

Initially spiral movement of air masses, then the cold front pushes under the warm front

Warm air front

The power of cyclones comes from the heat that is released when enormous quantities of water condense. In this process the rising air cools, and condensed water vapour forms towering thunderclouds. The air of the cyclone rotates anti-clockwise.

Phenomena in the Sky

By watching the weather, it is possible to experience a variety of phenomena in the sky that are not only colourful but also have a geometrically exact shape. The explanation for these phenomena lies in rays of the sun, which fall on molecules of air, ice crystals or raindrops when they pass through the atmosphere. The bending of the rays by these components of the atmosphere causes reflections or refraction, and the results elicit admiring looks and exclamations. We see these phenomena as rainbows, mirages, polar lights or aureoles.

Comets are a completely different kind of heavenly phenomenon. Suddenly they appear from nowhere, and for weeks we see a comet and its long tail in the night sky, but just as quickly they disappear again somewhere into the depths of space.

Light is refracted and separated into spectral colours

Rays of the sun

Rainbow

Sun

Rain

Drops of water

A rainbow is formed when the sun shines through clouds while it is still raining. Each raindrop refracts the sun's rays falling on it, first when entering the drop and a second time when emerging from the drop. This takes place at different angles. At the same time the sunlight is separated into its spectral colours as if through a prism. Each colour leaves the raindrop at a different angle. The combination of this process repeated many millions of times gives rise to the rainbow.

53,2°
50,2°
42,2°
40,4°

Rainbows

A rainbow must be one of the best-known optical phenomena in the atmosphere. It is caused by reflection and refraction of light in raindrops.

When a ray of the sun falls on a drop of water, it undergoes refraction on entering the raindrop and is reflected by the surface of the raindrop. When emerging from the raindrop, the ray is refracted for a second time. This takes place at different angles.

Not all wavelengths are refracted to an equal extent. The blue and violet components of light are refracted more strongly than the red ones. In this way white light is separated into its spectral colours, and each colour emerges from the raindrop at a different angle, i. e. shades of blue at a different angle from shades of red. Around each individual raindrop, a cone of rays is created. This is visible to the observer as a rainbow in glowing violet, blue and red colours, with

reds always formed at an angle of 42.2° to the line from the sun to the observer's head, and violet at 40.4°.

The intensity of the colours depends on the size of the raindrops. Very small raindrops create overlapping colours, leading to orange and pink tones. From the ground only a part of this circular figure can be made out – the reason why it is called a rainbow. To the observer sitting in an aircraft, the whole circle would be visible when the sun is in the right position.

Mirages

A mirage is created by the refraction and reflection of light in layers of air with different densities. Mirages have given many thirsty desert travellers the illusion that a lake or river must be extremely close.

If a ray of the sun in the atmosphere falls through layers of air with higher density, it is bent or diverted as it passes through each layer. This process is known as refraction.

To the observer the rays seem to be moving in a straight line. When the ground is extremely hot, distant objects are shifted downwards. On an asphalt road, the optical shift of blue sky can make it seem like water, which disappears into nothing as the observer approaches.

In the desert even objects that lie behind the horizon, such as trees, buildings or landmarks, can be reflected so as to appear to be close.

Polar Lights

Polar lights occur in the upper atmosphere, especially in the polar regions.

In the northern hemisphere they are also called northern lights or aurora borealis, in the southern hemisphere southern lights or aurora australis.

Polar lights are caused by energy-rich particles of solar wind, which are captured by the electromagnetic field of the earth. At enormous speed protons and electrons collide with oxygen and nitrogen molecules in the upper atmosphere. They force the electrons out of the molecules and increase their energetic charge.

When the molecules return to their normal state, the light phenomena occur.

Polar lights often happen at altitudes of about 100 km. They are especially frequent in an ellipse-shaped region around the poles at a distance of about 23° from the poles.

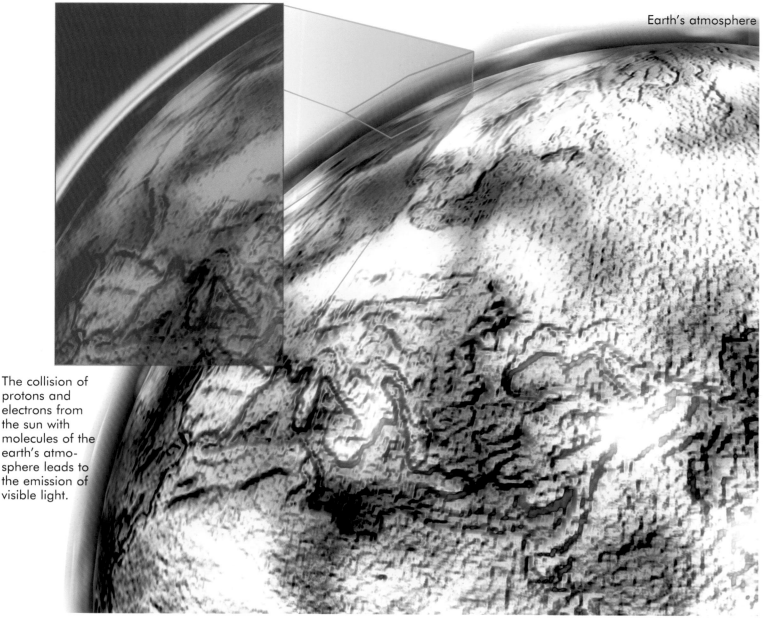

Earth's atmosphere

The collision of protons and electrons from the sun with molecules of the earth's atmosphere leads to the emission of visible light.

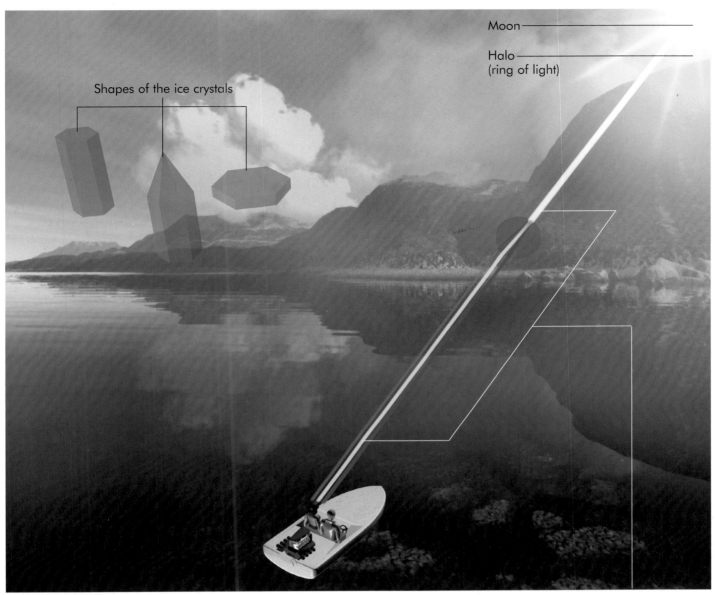

Moon

Halo
(ring of light)

Shapes of the ice crystals

When moonlight passes through ice crystals in the air, a ring of light sometimes forms around the moon. It is known as a halo. It is a result of refraction or reflection by the ice crystals in the atmosphere. Sometimes haloes form around the sun, too.

Reflection or refraction of light by ice crystals

Haloes

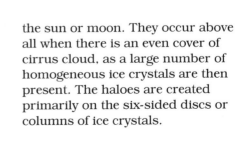

Haloes are among the most spectacular happenings in the sky. They arise through refraction or reflection of a light source by ice crystals in the atmosphere.

Haloes appear as white or, less commonly, coloured rings around the sun or moon. They occur above all when there is an even cover of cirrus cloud, as a large number of homogeneous ice crystals are then present. The haloes are created primarily on the six-sided discs or columns of ice crystals.

Aureoles

The images around the sun and moon that we call aureoles or coronae are caused not by refraction of rays of light, as in the case of rainbows or haloes, but by diffraction of light rays.

When light waves collide with droplets of clouds, they are diffracted to varying degrees. This produces a coloured ring of light around the sun or moon, the radius of which depends on the size of the cloud droplets. This ring is called an aureole.

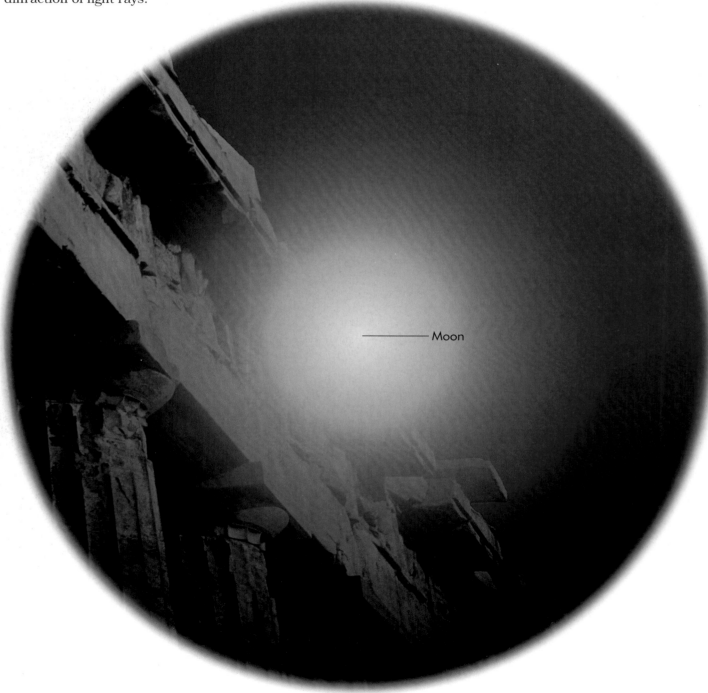

———— Moon

Meteors/Meteorites

Meteorite Impact

Surface of the earth   Meteorites (fragments falling on the surface of the earth)   Meteors (visible as shooting stars when they burn up)

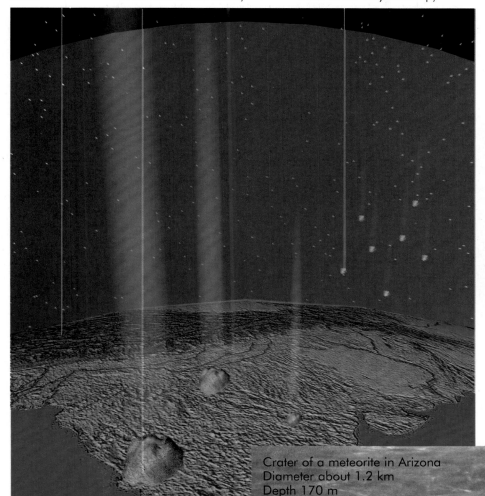

Meteors are pieces of rock and iron that spin about in the atmosphere, where most of them burn up. On clear starry nights we can enjoy this spectacle in the form of shooting stars. However, if meteors pass through the atmosphere, they fall on the earth's surface as meteorites and produce craters of varying sizes. Most meteorites plunge unnoticed into the sea.

Iron meteorite found on earth with size comparison

Crater of a meteorite in Arizona
Diameter about 1.2 km
Depth 170 m

Estimated size of meteorite: diameter 30 m, weight 150,000 t

On its orbit around the sun, the earth passes each year into regions where very many particles and great amounts of dust are swirling around. If these particles come into contact with the earth's atmosphere at speeds of up to 40 km/s, they burn up in the upper layers of the atmosphere and can be seen like a glowing ball as a meteor or shooting star.

Exact analysis of orbits has shown a connection between these phenomena and comets. It is thus obvious that meteors are waste products from comets. If a piece of material survives its collision with the atmosphere intact and hits the surface of the earth, it is called a meteorite. This is estimated to happen somewhere on earth about 50 times each day. However, most meteorites fall into the sea. If they break up during the fall, the fragments come down as thousands of stones. 90% of all meteorites consist mainly of stone, about 5% of iron and the remainder of combinations of stone and iron. The largest known iron meteorite is called the Hoba meteorite. It weighs 54 tonnes and lies in Namibia.

Comets

Comets have always made a great impression on humanity. They used to be regarded as omens of misfortune.

Today it is believed that millions of comets move around the sun in a comet cloud many thousands of times further away than Neptune, the planet most distant from the sun.

In essence a comet consists of its head and its tail. The nucleus is 1 to 50 km in diameter and can be composed of several pieces. These pieces are made up of dark dust, ice and organic compounds. If a comet approaches the sun, it glows a faint blue colour and is gradually warmed in the inner part of the solar system. The ice evaporating on the surface forms a covering known as a coma, which surrounds the nucleus like an atmosphere. The electrically charged solar wind pushes gases out of this coma. The gases then form a tail pointing away from the sun and often millions of kilometres long. The particles of dust are also pushed away from the comet, so that a second tail is formed. As dust moves more slowly than gas, this tail has somewhat curved appearance.

The comet loses many particles of dust during its course around the sun. If by chance the earth passes through this region, the atmosphere captures these particles and burns them up. This is the process visible to us as shooting stars.

Astronomers divide comets into two groups according to the duration of their orbit around the sun: long-period comets are thought to derive from a comet cloud known as an Oort cloud. They have orbits lasting more than 200 years and highly eccentric paths.

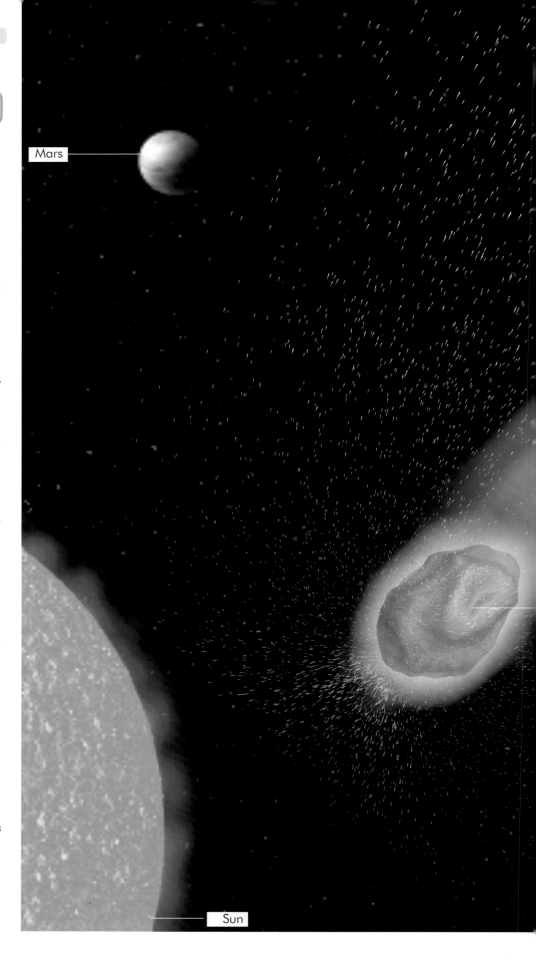

Mars

Sun

Tail of gas

Jupiter

Tail of dust

Comet

Earth

Moon

Comets are like dirty snowballs at the edge of the solar system. They are composed of icy dust particles and gas. If they approach the sun, part of the ice surrounding them evaporates. The comet is then enclosed in a mantle of gas, which is pulled away by the electrically charged solar wind. A long tail of gas pointing away from the sun forms in this way. Dust particles are also forced away and form a second, slightly curved tail of dust.

Short-period comets have orbits lasting less than 200 years. They probably come from the Kuiper belt, which is located on the far side of the orbital path of Neptune. Comet Encke is one of the short-period comets. It takes only 3.3 years to travel around the sun and can be watched permanently through a telescope.

Probably the best-known comet of recent decades is Halley's comet. It was named after the English astronomer Edmond Halley, who had predicted its return. During his observations, Halley came to be convinced that the bright comets seen in 1531, 1607 and 1682 must have been one and the same comet, and he correctly predicted its return for 1758.

By using historical records, Halley's comet has now been traced back as far as the year 240 BC. When it appeared in 1986 its nucleus was investigated for the first time by the space probe Giotto from a distance of only 600 km.

Threats to the Environment

In recent decades many protective measures have been taken to limit the extent of natural catastrophes as far as possible.

There are now alarm systems in the Pacific that can give early warning of tsunamis, the great waves that suddenly inflict destruction on coastal regions. Efforts are being made in Japan, China and the United States to predict impending earthquakes with a network of observation posts. Areas threatened by flooding are excluded from the very beginning from plans for construction work, in order to prevent catastrophes at a later date.

However, a threat to the earth still exists: humanity itself! Poisonous substances in industrial and agricultural waste products pollute the soil, the groundwater and the seas.

During the production of many synthetic materials, highly poisonous gases are emitted that reinforce the greenhouse effect and cause smog. Whole areas of countryside are deforested and rivers made biologically dead by the increase of acid rain caused by the emission of CO_2 from cars and coal-burning stoves.

In order to avert an environmental disaster, it is not only necessary to change our ways of thinking, but also for each individual to act in an ecologically aware manner.

Acid Rain

Sulphur dioxide and carbon dioxide are components of unpolluted rain. Rain is naturally acidic, a consequence of the sulphur emissions of volcanoes but also of the composition of air. Air contains traces of dioxides in the form of gas.

The natural acid content of rain does not damage the environment. However, the situation has changed with increasing industrialisation. When fossil fuels such as coal and oil are burned, additional sulphur dioxide is released. The wind spreads the dioxides, which are converted into sulphates and nitrates by the sun's rays. Acids containing nitrogen and sulphuric acids then collect in clouds and return to the earth's surface via rain or other precipitation. In this way the acidity of rain increases by up to 500 times compared to its natural state.

For a time the soil can resist these harmful influences if neutralising chemicals such as calcium (for example in limestone) are present. Nutrients such as magnesium or calcium are leached from the soil by acid rain, however, leading to damage to the trees.

Coniferous forests are especially badly affected. The situation is aggravated in winter when acidic snow lies on trees. As a result, nutrients are drawn directly from the needles of the trees. When the snow melts, the acidic water goes into the soil and damages the roots. In this way trees are harmed by poisons in the environment. If other damaging factors such as pests or periods of drought are added to this, the weakened trees die.

Acid rain affects not only trees, but also buildings. The stones of historic buildings can even be eaten away by a high acid content.

When the bed of a lake is rocky, the sulphuric acid cannot be neutralised due to a lack of calcium. In consequence the lake becomes acidic, leading to damage to plants and fish.

Many areas of European forest have been affected by this damage to trees. A change has taken place as a result of increasing environmental awareness, the installation of filters in industrial plants for removing nitrogen and sulphur and the inclusion of catalytic converters in cars. In South America, Africa, Asia and the Indian subcontinent, by contrast, industrial growth is proceeding so quickly, with environmental regulations often being ignored, that the effects of acid rain are particularly noticeable there.

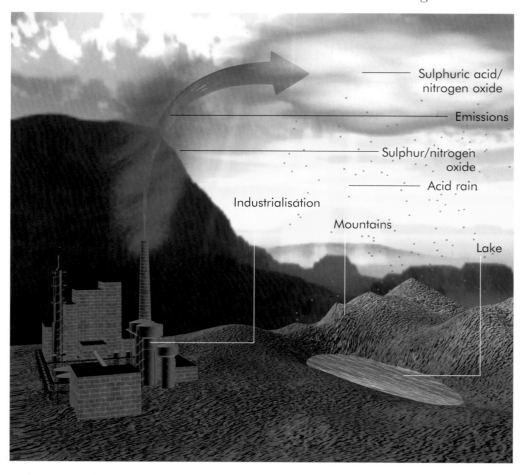

Sulphuric acid/
nitrogen oxide

Emissions

Sulphur/nitrogen
oxide

Acid rain

Industrialisation

Mountains

Lake

Acid rain is caused by the general spread of industrialisation. When fuel is burned, increased quantities of sulphur and nitrogen oxides are taken into the air. In combination with sunlight and the atmosphere, they produce raised levels of sulphuric acids and nitrogen oxides. These poisonous substances return to the earth's surface with the rain. The forests are damaged when these substances are deposited on trees or seep into the ground.

Greenhouse Effect

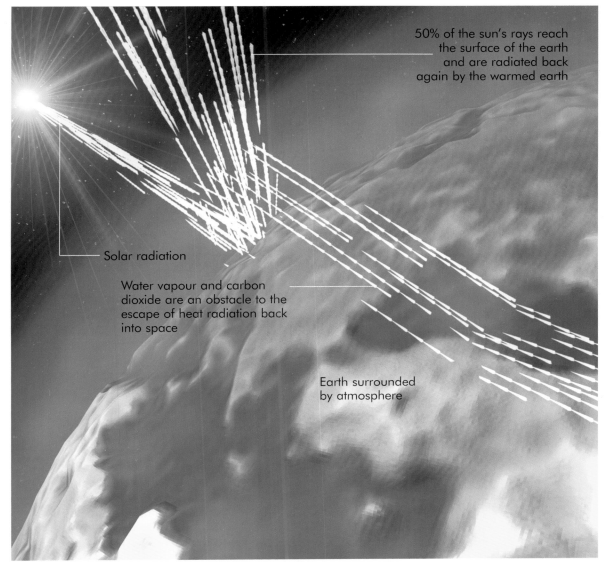

50% of the sun's rays reach the surface of the earth and are radiated back again by the warmed earth

Solar radiation

Water vapour and carbon dioxide are an obstacle to the escape of heat radiation back into space

Earth surrounded by atmosphere

The earth is warmed by the sun but radiates this heat back through the atmosphere into space. However, this process can take place only in part, because gases which also rise from the earth such as water vapour, carbon dioxide and methane absorb the radiated heat and transmit it back to earth. This process leads to the greenhouse effect.

Life would not be possible on our planet without the natural greenhouse effect. Sunlight can penetrate a glasshouse practically unhindered and warm it. However, the radiated warmth that is produced cannot escape again through the glass without hindrance, and as a result heat is stored. A similar process takes place in the atmosphere around us. It is composed of various gases: 78% nitrogen, 21% oxygen, 0.9% argon, 0.04% carbon dioxide and trace gases.

50% of the sun's radiation reaches the surface of the earth unobstructed and warms it. The heated earth radiates warmth back again, but as in a greenhouse this heat radiation cannot simply escape through the atmosphere into space, but is held back. Water vapour and carbon dioxide are mainly responsible for this. They absorb the radiated warmth and return it to the earth. The average temperature on earth is at present about +15 °C. Without the greenhouse effect, the average temperature would also be 15 °C – but with a minus sign in front, i. e. –15 °C.

Human activity has led to an increase in the greenhouse effect over the last decades. Industry, traffic and agriculture have caused a rise in the greenhouse gases. These gases reduce the escape of heat radiation into space and radiate a part of it back to the earth. The more greenhouse gases such as carbon dioxide or methane are present, the more heat radiation remains in circulation between the earth and the atmosphere. The result is a slow but steady warming.

Climatic Change

When unusual weather phenomena occur, one question is soon raised: has the climate of our earth changed significantly in recent decades?

Following a cooling of the Atlantic and a fall in temperatures in the northern polar region in the 1960s, some scientists announced the beginning of a new "little ice age". These observations alone were not sufficient, however, as proof of a general cooling of the earth.

Today the issue under discussion is to what extent there will be global warming in the coming decades. Warming could be the result of human intervention, by means of

which more and more greenhouse gases such as hydrofluorocarbons, methane and carbon dioxide are released into the atmosphere (greenhouse effect). Natural events too, such as a shift in the position of ocean currents or a change in the

Rain of Gases and Ash during Volcanic Eruptions

flow of ice into the ocean around Greenland, could have an effect on the circulation of air and thus influence the climate. Altogether there has been only a slight rise in temperature so far.

Climate researchers must look for evidence for a change in global temperatures by using the climatic data of the last decades from all over the world. This includes interpretation of particular events such as droughts, cool and rainy summers or mild winter temperatures. This analysis, and predictions of climatic changes and their effects in the coming years, are important areas of work for climate research.

Disturbance of the Natural Equilibrium

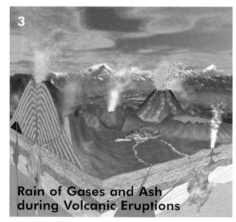

Destruction of the Ozone Layer

Fig. 1–5
The earth's climate in the future is dependent on various factors. Human intervention such as high energy consumption and the consequent high level of emissions into the atmosphere could lead to changes in the reflection of sunlight. In the long term this would result in global warming. On the other hand, natural events such as volcanic eruptions could alter the chemical equilibrium. Their gases and ash create a shield in the atmosphere that allows less sunlight to reach the surface of the earth.

Emission of Poisons

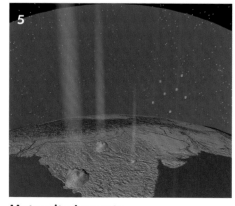

Meteorite Impacts

Greenhouse Effect

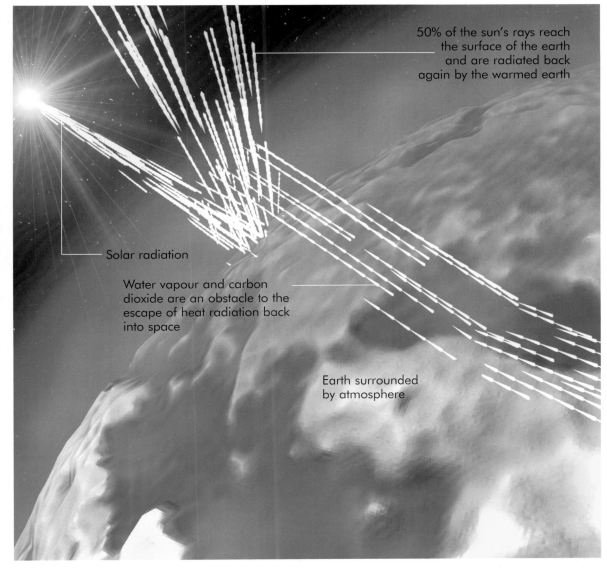

50% of the sun's rays reach the surface of the earth and are radiated back again by the warmed earth

Solar radiation

Water vapour and carbon dioxide are an obstacle to the escape of heat radiation back into space

Earth surrounded by atmosphere

The earth is warmed by the sun but radiates this heat back through the atmosphere into space. However, this process can take place only in part, because gases which also rise from the earth such as water vapour, carbon dioxide and methane absorb the radiated heat and transmit it back to earth. This process leads to the greenhouse effect.

Life would not be possible on our planet without the natural greenhouse effect. Sunlight can penetrate a glasshouse practically unhindered and warm it. However, the radiated warmth that is produced cannot escape again through the glass without hindrance, and as a result heat is stored. A similar process takes place in the atmosphere around us. It is composed of various gases: 78% nitrogen, 21% oxygen, 0.9% argon, 0.04% carbon dioxide and trace gases.

50% of the sun's radiation reaches the surface of the earth unobstructed and warms it. The heated earth radiates warmth back again, but as in a greenhouse this heat radiation cannot simply escape through the atmosphere into space, but is held back. Water vapour and carbon dioxide are mainly responsible for this. They absorb the radiated warmth and return it to the earth. The average temperature on earth is at present about +15 °C. Without the greenhouse effect, the average temperature would also be 15 °C – but with a minus sign in front, i. e. –15 °C.

Human activity has led to an increase in the greenhouse effect over the last decades. Industry, traffic and agriculture have caused a rise in the greenhouse gases. These gases reduce the escape of heat radiation into space and radiate a part of it back to the earth. The more greenhouse gases such as carbon dioxide or methane are present, the more heat radiation remains in circulation between the earth and the atmosphere. The result is a slow but steady warming.

Destruction
of the ozone layer

Earth

The influence of human activities was gradually destroying the ozone layer in our atmosphere. The main harmful substances are hydrofluorocarbons, nitrogen oxides and sulphuric acids.

Hole in the Ozone Layer

Ozone is a relatively rare gas and a poisonous form of oxygen. It consists of three atoms in one molecule. In oxygen, by contrast, there are only two atoms per molecule.

Ozone is present throughout the atmosphere to an altitude of about 50 km. The layer with the highest concentration of ozone (ozone layer) lies at a height of about 25 km above sea level at low latitudes. Towards the polar regions the height of the ozone layer decreases.

The short-wave component of ultraviolet rays causes oxygen to be converted into ozone by a photochemical reaction. As a result the ultraviolet radiation, which damages cells, is mostly absorbed.

The use of hydrofluorocarbons as aerosol propellants and in the production of foam results in damage to the ozone layer. Ozone is able to oxidise hydrofluorocarbons and in doing to is reduced to oxygen again. Ultraviolet rays in concentrations dangerous to humans and animals

can reach the earth's surface when the ozone layer is damaged.

Hydrofluorocarbons have a very long lifetime and can result in damage to the ozone layer many years after their release. At low temperatures this process of damage is especially obvious. A noticeable depletion of ozone has been observed in the Antarctic winter since the early 1980s. This condition is known as the ozone hole. Today, the ozone layer is expected to recover in coming decades.

Changes to the Earth's Surface

The external appearance of the earth's land masses is in a state of continual change. If forests are cut down for their timber or cleared for agriculture, whole areas of land can eventually become barren.

The roots of trees hold the soil together and store water. In this way they prevent precipitation and wind from eroding the soil. Moreover, as a result rain does not seep into the earth, but is put back into the air through the leaves.

In the past fields were not used in a balanced way, as the cereal planted was always the same type. Agricultural land was also over-fertilised in order to obtain better and higher yields. The result was that the soil dried out or became unusable.

The construction of dams and regulation of rivers to make them navigable alters the environment. The face of the earth is also changed by the extraction of minerals, which lowers the ground level, over-grazing by herds of animals and road-building.

Efforts are also being made, however, to make a favourable impact on the appearance of the landscape. In North Africa and the Near East projects have begun to make infertile land suitable for crops by means of sophisticated irrigation systems. Reforestation is going ahead in many places and, especially in the Netherlands, attempts are being made to create new land with gigantic dykes.

More than anything else, however, it is the forces of nature that change the face of the earth. Climate changes subject the land to different temperatures. Wind and rain erode the soil. Deposits of sediment, weathering and erosion create new landscapes. Lastly plate tectonics, i. e. the shift of land masses, throws up ranges of mountains and pushes continents into different climatic zones. These changes to the surface of the earth proceed constantly, but very slowly.

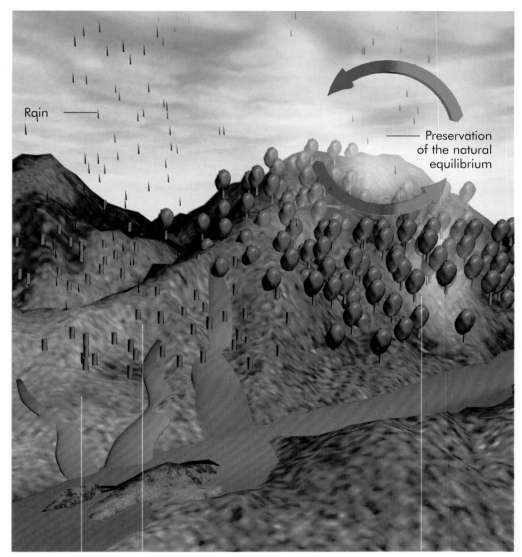

Rain

Preservation of the natural equilibrium

Land becomes barren

Erosion and weathering

Soil well-provided with roots and rich in nutrients

If large areas of forest are cut down, the open spaces are exposed to weathering and erosion. The land inevitably becomes barren. In contrast to this, the natural equilibrium is preserved in a forested area. The soil is held together by roots and is thus better able to absorb water. Water is returned to its natural cycle through the leaves.

Climatic Change

When unusual weather phenomena occur, one question is soon raised: has the climate of our earth changed significantly in recent decades?

Following a cooling of the Atlantic and a fall in temperatures in the northern polar region in the 1960s, some scientists announced the beginning of a new "little ice age". These observations alone were not sufficient, however, as proof of a general cooling of the earth.

Today the issue under discussion is to what extent there will be global warming in the coming decades. Warming could be the result of human intervention, by means of which more and more greenhouse gases such as hydrofluorocarbons, methane and carbon dioxide are released into the atmosphere (greenhouse effect). Natural events too, such as a shift in the position of ocean currents or a change in the

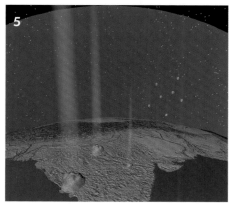

Rain of Gases and Ash during Volcanic Eruptions

flow of ice into the ocean around Greenland, could have an effect on the circulation of air and thus influence the climate. Altogether there has been only a slight rise in temperature so far.

Climate researchers must look for evidence for a change in global temperatures by using the climatic data of the last decades from all over the world. This includes interpretation of particular events such as droughts, cool and rainy summers or mild winter temperatures. This analysis, and predictions of climatic changes and their effects in the coming years, are important areas of work for climate research.

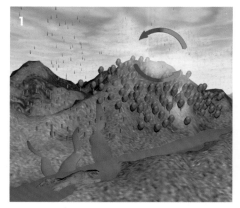

Disturbance of the Natural Equilibrium

Emission of Poisons

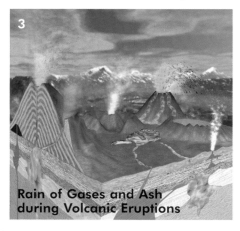

Fig. 1–5

The earth's climate in the future is dependent on various factors. Human intervention such as high energy consumption and the consequent high level of emissions into the atmosphere could lead to changes in the reflection of sunlight. In the long term this would result in global warming. On the other hand, natural events such as volcanic eruptions could alter the chemical equilibrium. Their gases and ash create a shield in the atmosphere that allows less sunlight to reach the surface of the earth.

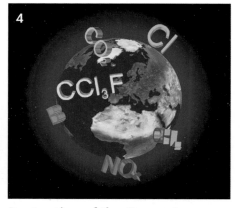

Destruction of the Ozone Layer

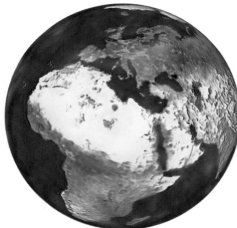

Meteorite Impacts

Smog

The term "smog" is formed from the words "smoke" and "fog". The use of coal with a high sulphur content in most London homes once led to the first appearance of this phenomenon, a thick pall of fumes over the city consisting of smoke, gas emissions and dirt.

Today smog is created in almost every large city. It is caused by industrial emissions, the burning of fossil fuels and car exhaust fumes.

During the winter the smog often is especially dense. The reason for this is that inversion layers prevent circulation of air. Colder air close to the ground is blocked in by warmer layers above it. These inversions usually arise around areas of high pressure. Gas emissions cause water vapour to condense, leading to the smog that threatens the environment.

City Climate

Carbon monoxide

Nitrogen oxide

Benzene

Smog

The moist air then contains nitrogen oxide and sulphur dioxide. The acidic droplets produced in this way cause damage to the buildings and vegetation that they fall on.

Humans absorb the poisonous substances when they breathe. This frequently leads to bronchial complaints and illnesses of the lungs. It is not unusual for these illnesses to be chronic among city dwellers. Children and old people are especially affected.

In order to prevent a build-up of pollutants, the use of private vehicles is prohibited when there is a smog alarm.

In this case even healthy people should avoid going out into the polluted air. At the very least strenuous physical activity should be avoided, as it is then necessary to breathe in more deeply.

Planet Earth

During the evolution of the universe, gigantic astronomical structures were formed: the so-called super star clusters, consisting of several thousand galaxies with several million billion suns. Our galaxy, the Milky Way, is part of a group of about 30 galaxies of varying size. Our solar system is rotating in one of the spiral arms far away from the centre of the Milky Way. Eight planets, accompanied by moons, comets and asteroids, revolve around the sun on their own orbits. Mercury, Venus, Earth and Mars are the inner planets, Jupiter, Saturn, Uranus and Neptune are the outer ones.

Our earth has a diameter of about 13,000 km and orbits at a distance of about 150 million km from the sun. The earth is protected from the danger of the sun's rays, particles of solar wind, dust from space and meteorites by its magnetic field and atmosphere. As part of our system of planets, the earth rotates on its own axis once every 24 hours. In the course of a year it travels an elliptical path about one billion kilometres long. The tilt of the earth's axis (23.5°) gives rise to the seasons during the annual orbit around the sun. As a result of gravity, the moon is bound to the earth. It rotates around its own axis about once every 28 days while orbiting the earth.

The evolution of the earth can be seen in the composition and structure of many different types of rock. Fossils too are helpful here. Discoveries made so far indicate that the earth is about 4.5 billion years old.

1

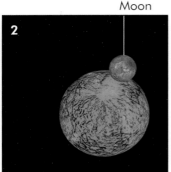

2

Moon

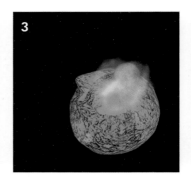

3

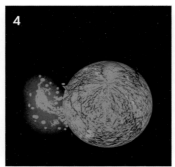

4

5

Earth

The Earth and the Moon

Of the planets with a solid interior orbiting the sun, the earth is the largest. Its diameter at the equator measures 12,756 km. Seen from space, earth with its oceans and atmosphere appears as the "blue planet". The surface of the earth consists of rocks. At the deepest depressions on its surface, two-thirds of the earth is covered by the water of the oceans, as the distance from the sun is just great enough for the water neither to freeze nor evaporate.

On the higher ground of the earth's surface, humans live on seven continents: Africa, North America, South America, Asia, Australia, Europe and the Antarctic, which is covered with ice.

The atmosphere surrounding the earth, which consists of 78% nitro-gen and 21% oxygen, shields it from the heat and ultraviolet rays of the sun.

Fragments of matter spinning through space are normally burned up in the atmosphere and do not reach the earth. The magnetic field around the earth protects life from the electric particles of the solar wind. Our earth is an active planet. Changes are constantly taking place on it as a result of continental drift, the oceans, the atmosphere and life itself. This situation exists nowhere else in the solar system.

The moon with its many craters, the results of meteorite impacts, is our constant companion in space. The moon has about one quarter of the earth's diameter and is often described along with the earth as a double planet. The large mass of the moon is the cause of tides.

However, this mass is not large enough for the moon to hold an atmosphere. The temperature is about +130 °C on the day side and −150 °C on the dark side of the moon. It is thought that the moon was born about 50 to 100 million years after the earth was formed through a collision between the earth and a planet as big as Mars. The moon is believed to have originated in the fragments from the collision. Since cooling down it has revolved around the earth.

View of the Earth from the Moon

Surface of the moon   Earth

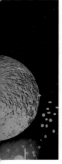
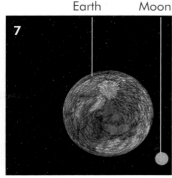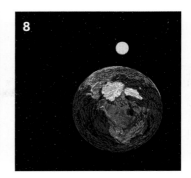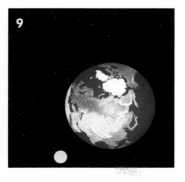

Earth   Moon

6 7 8 9

agments
f a planet

Fig. 1–9 Theory on the Origin of the Moon
One of the many theories about the origin of the moon states that the earth was hit by another planet about 50 to 100 million years after it was formed. When this happened, the iron cores of the two planets fused, and at the same time parts of the fragments were thrown off, forming the moon. It gradually cooled down and since then has orbited the earth. The relatively low proportion of metal in the moon and its low density are arguments in favour of this theory.

The 800 km wide core of the moon, which is presumed to consist of molten iron, is covered by a thick mantle of rock. The side of the moon turned away from the earth is a landscape of craters that points to a large number of meteorite impacts. On the nearer side of the moon, the side facing the earth, there are deep basins, the "seas". Researchers originally thought that the dark patches on the moon were expanses of water. Areas of high ground, full of craters, lie around the seas.

The round "seas" as well as the craters are signs of collisions with other heavenly bodies – collisions that must have been so powerful that the moon's crust broke open and allowed masses of lava to flow from inside.

The moon rotates around its own axis once in about every 27.8 days. This is exactly the amount of time it needs to orbit around the earth, which means that the side of the moon facing the earth is always the same side. Despite this, the moon seems to us to have a changing appearance. The reason for this is that it is illuminated by the sun differently every night and so reflects light back to earth in a different way.

This gives rise to different phases of the moon: at new moon we do not see it at all, because no sunlight falls on the side facing us. In the course of the next 28 days the moon first waxes (increases), then wanes (decreases). We use the term full moon for the time when the earth is positioned exactly between the sun and moon.

The side of the moon facing us is fully illuminated. The situation when the moon moves into the shadow of the earth and is no longer visible is known as an eclipse of the moon.

Phases of the Moon

Earth

The Lunar Cycle/Phases of the Moon
The moon revolves around the earth in a 28-day cycle. At the same time it rotates on its own axis once. New moon is when the moon lies between the earth and the sun. The side facing the earth is then dark. After this, the moon gradually waxes. First of all only a crescent-shaped section is illuminated and then a half-moon, until finally at full moon the whole front side of the moon lit by the sun can be seen. In this phase the moon is behind the earth but not in its shadow. As it proceeds on its course, only three quarters of the waning moon is visible on earth. After that only a crescent appears, and finally nothing at all – the new moon phase has come round again.

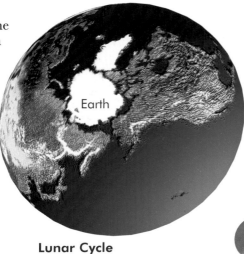

Earth

Lunar Cycle

New moon

Sun

The Earth's History

The age of the earth is estimated at over 4.5 billion years. The appearance of our planet has continually changed in the course of this inconceivable period of time. Not only living nature, but also rocks and minerals are subject to cycles. Mountain ranges are created and then levelled again, continents drift, living organisms evolve and then become extinct.

How is it possible to allocate individual changes to a particular period in the development of the earth? Because we know how quickly (or better: how slowly) radioactive elements decay, when investigating layers of rock we can reach conclusions about the age of the deposits by reference to these elements. Fossils are also found in layers of sediment. By identifying the age of the fossils we can also tell how old the surrounding layer of rock is.

Precambrian

The first 4 billion years, the early period in the history of the earth, are known as the Precambrian. Only fossils from the end of this period have been found. Nevertheless it can be said that the first simple forms of life emerged at this time.

Because the earth's crust, which consists of rock, is continually changing through sedimentation, erosion, deformation, melting and recrystallisation, and the original formations therefore hardly exist any more, little can be said about this time, by far the longest period in the history of the earth.

Single-cell organisms first appeared about 3.5 billion years

ago. This is thought to have occurred through the spontaneous fusion of molecules.

The cloud of cosmic dust from which the earth formed was at first unsuitable for the emergence of life, as no oxygen was present. Moreover, the atmosphere was not able to absorb the sun's ultraviolet rays.

The single-cell organisms, consisting of chains of molecules, were present for about 2 billion years. These first forms of life were then able to carry out photosynthesis and so supplied a prerequisite for the production of oxygen. The first multi-cell organisms formed about 2 billion years ago.

Paleozoic

The first part of the following eon (an eon is the largest category of time of the earth's history), the Paleozoic, was the Cambrian period. Multi-cell organisms evolved into molluscs. However, it is a rather unusual stroke of luck for paleontologists, the scientists concerned with forms of life in earlier stages of the earth's history, for fossils of these molluscs to be

found. Normally only the hard parts such as armour, bones or snail shells are preserved. In the Cambrian period trilobites were widespread. As they did not live for a long period, rock formations of this period can be classified when fossils of this type are discovered.

The next periods of the Paleozoic were the Ordovician and the Silurian. Large parts of the land mass were flooded by sea. At this time

Era	Period
	Quatern
Cenozoic	Tertiar
	Cretaceou
	Jurassic
Mesozoic	Triassic
	Permian
	Carbonifer
	Devonian
Paleozoic	Silurian
	Ordivician
	Cambrian
Precambrian	

Epoch	Beginning
Holocene	
Pleistocene	0.01
Pliocene	1.6
Miocene	5.3
Oligocene	23
Eocene	34
Paleocene	53
	65
	135
	205
	250
	300
	355
	410
	435
	510
	570

Millions of years

4600

Mesozoic

After the Permian came the Mesozoic, the middle period in earth's history. It is subdivided into Triassic, Jurassic and Cretaceous. From now on and for a long period of time, life on earth was dominated by the dinosaurs, a word meaning "fearsome lizards". Reptiles evolved not only into dinosaurs, however, but also into birds and mammals.

A great part of what today is Europe was flooded. Dry land did not return until the Cretaceous period. This flooding explains why marine fossils are found in mountains.

The Cenozoic, the most recent eon in the history of the earth, began 65 million years ago. Different types of warm-blooded mammals took over the world. The dinosaurs, on the other hand, died out within a relatively short period of time. This happened between the Cretaceous and the Paleocene period, a time of climatic change. There may be different or additional reasons, such as the impact of a meteorite, for the extinction of many kinds of reptiles and the dinosaurs. The Alps and the Pyrenees, and in Africa the Atlas mountains, formed in the Tertiary period.

The Tertiary was followed by the Quaternary period. The earth became much cooler and the first ice ages began. Over 20 periods when the ice advanced and retreated have occurred during the last 2 million years. The effect of the ice age was that large glaciers advanced into Europe, leaving moraines behind them. Between the ice ages the temperature rose, and the thaw led to flooding.

The evolution of the human ancestors began in Africa more than 6 million years ago with Australopithecus, from which Homo erectus and later today's Homo sapiens evolved.

the first vertebrates, such as armour fish, evolved. A great mountain range stretching from Scandinavia to Scotland was formed. Then came the Devonian period, with the first land plants and the first ancestors of amphibians. Following the expansion of the surface of the oceans, mountains appeared and extended the land mass in the Carboniferous period.

The first forests grew, and remain of great importance to us today. Our coal was formed from them in the course of millions of years. Insects appeared, and with the reptiles the first land vertebrates evolved. The Paleozoic ended more than 250 million years ago with the Permian period.

Seasons

Spring, summer, winter and autumn are mainly felt in the temperate zones of the earth. At the north and south pole there are only two seasons, the polar night and the polar day. The seasons of the year can also be characterised as dry and rainy seasons.

The earth is tilted at an angle of 23.5° to the perpendicular of its orbit. It rotates about its own axis once every 24 hours. During the orbit of the earth around the sun over a period of 365.25 days, the angle at which the sun's rays meet the earth (the position of the sun) changes. In winter the sun's rays

meet the earth at a low angle. Their warmth is spread over a greater area, which means that it is colder than in summer. In the northern hemisphere four astronomical seasons are distinguished:

- March 21 to June 20. Spring.
- June 21 to September 22. Summer.
- September 23 to December 20. Autumn.
- December 21 to March 20. Winter.

On March 23 and September 23 the day and night are equally long (equinox). The longest day and shortest night falls on June 21

(solstice). In the southern hemisphere it is autumn during our spring, and winter during our summer. The seasons do not change abruptly on the dates fixed by astronomers. The reason for the slow transitions is that the position of the sun and the number of hours of sunshine are not the only factors determining the weather.

Ocean currents, mountains and plains also influence the seasons. The largest differences in temperature between summer and winter are in Siberia. Here there can be a fluctuation between −75 °C in winter and +40 °C in summer.

Start of Spring

March 21

Start of Summer

June 21

The Sun's Rays
The earth revolves around the sun on its elliptical orbit once every year. It is 152 million km from the sun in the northern summer and 147 million km in the winter. However, the earth's axis is not perpendicular to this elliptical orbit, but tilted at an angle of 23.5° to the perpendicular. This fact determines the seasons. When the sun shines vertically at the equator, the date is March 23, the beginning of spring. On June 21 the sun is vertical at the northern

December 31

Angle of the earth's axis to its orbit

Seasons

In the course of the earth's orbit around the sun, there are changes in the angle at which the sun's rays meet the earth. In summer the sun stands higher in the sky and it is therefore warmer. In winter the warmth of the sun is spread over a larger area, because its rays fall on the earth at a lower angle. It is therefore colder.

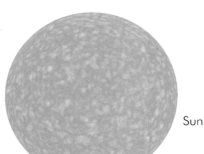

Sun

Earth

Start of Autumn

September 23

Start of Winter

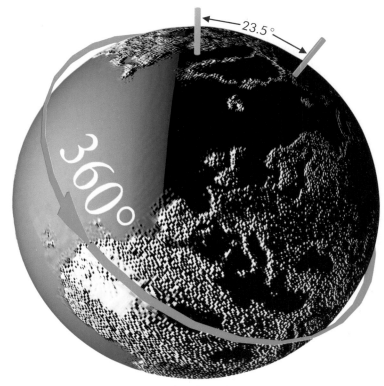

December 21

tropic or Tropic of Cancer, latitude 23.5° north. This is the start of summer in the northern hemisphere. On September 23 the sun is again vertical at the equator on the other side of the earth's orbit; this is the start of autumn. On December 21 the earth has travelled so far on its orbit around the sun that the sun shines vertically at the southern tropic or Tropic of Capricorn, latitude 23.5° south. In the northern hemisphere this is the start of winter.

Tides

As all the oceans are connected to each other, sea level is the same everywhere on the earth. Lakes or inland seas such as the Dead Sea can lie at a higher or lower level than sea level. Tides are responsible for changes in the sea level.

The tides are caused by the gravitational attraction of the sun and moon in connection with the centrifugal forces resulting from the rotation of the earth-moon system. On both sides of the earth, tidal swells result from the gravitational attraction of the moon and the centrifugal force from the rotation of earth and moon.

High tide and low tide follow a 28-day cycle. The effect is at its strongest (highest high tide, lowest low tide) when the sun, earth and moon are aligned. When the sun and moon are at right angles to each other, the attraction is less strong and tides are lower.

As the lunar day is 50 minutes longer than the solar day, the timing of the tides shifts every day. The gravitational attraction of the sun on the earth is about half as strong as that of the moon. These forces not only affect the tides, but also raise and lower the earth's crust by up to 60 cm. The difference between high and low tide, normally small on the open sea, is increased when masses of water are forced through straits.

In the Mediterranean Sea the tidal difference is hardly noticeable, as this body of water is almost entirely surrounded by land.

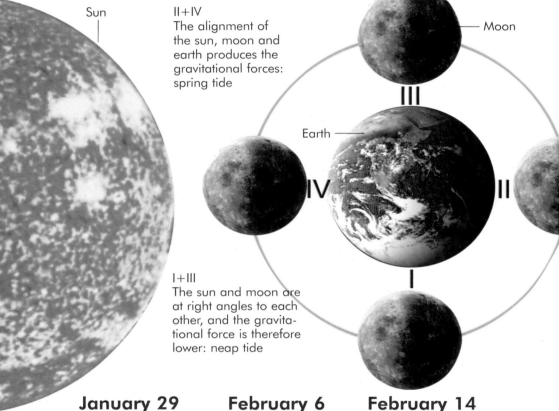

Sun

II+IV
The alignment of the sun, moon and earth produces the gravitational forces: spring tide

Moon

Earth

I+III
The sun and moon are at right angles to each other, and the gravitational force is therefore lower: neap tide

III

IV

II

I

January 29   February 6   February 14

8 m
7 m
6 m   Neap tide
5 m
4 m
3 m
2 m
1 m
0

Spring tide

Neap tide

Spring tide

Neap tide

min.   max.   min.   max.   min.

Day and Night

Day is the time between sunrise and sunset. On the first day of spring and autumn the day and night are exactly equal in length (12 hours each). In winter the days become shorter, in summer longer.

The nearer we come to the north or south pole, the greater the difference between daytime and night-time. At the poles it is daytime in the summer half year and night in the winter half year.

Day and night are the result of the rotation of the earth around its own axis. The side of the earth facing the sun is the day side, the side facing away is the night side.

By the way – scientists have discovered that 400 million years ago there were 400 days in the year. The reason for this was that the earth rotated faster at that period, making days and nights shorter.

The Universe

When we look around us in the universe, we see great numbers of heavenly bodies of different sizes. The earth is a small planet, if we consider only its size. However, a number of aspects of the earth make it special. The most obvious is the fact that there is life on earth. Further remarkable features are the earth's atmosphere and water as well as its self-renewing surface, the earth's crust.

During the course of human history, our view of the world has changed radically. This began with the geocentric world system, dating back to the Alexandrian astronomer Ptolemy (about AD 150). According to this system, the earth is the centre of space, and the sun and moon revolve around it. This assumption was maintained until the end of the Middle Ages, when Nicholas Copernicus (1473–1543) established the heliocentric system. He discovered that the earth revolves around the sun and that it also rotates around its own axis. The development of telescopes made better observation of the stars possible. As a consequence the discovery was made that the sun is not the central heavenly body either.

Our solar system is only a small part of the galaxy in which we are situated – the Milky Way. And this too is not the end of the story. In recent decades so many systems and galaxies have been discovered outside our galaxy that their numbers are now estimated at several billion.

Theories about the Origin of the Universe

Observations of the spectral lines of galaxies show a shift to the red end in comparison to light from the sun. This is known as the Doppler effect. This type of effect is familiar to us in acoustic terms. When a racing car approaches, its engine seems higher-pitched than when it is moving away from us. The pitch suddenly falls at the moment when it passes us. When it approaches us, the sound waves are compressed, and when it moves away, they are expanded. The same applies to light sources. If the source of light moves away, the waves become longer, which causes a shift to red. A red shift of the spectrum therefore means that the light sources, in this case galaxies, are moving away from us. The American astronomer Edwin Hubble (1889–1953) was the first to realise this. He also discovered that the further away a galaxy is, the higher the speed at which it recedes. This phenomenon is named after him as the Hubble effect. When the speed at which a galaxy moves away is divided by its distance, the result is the so-called Hubble constant.

The Hubble effect is an indication that the universe is expanding. By reversing time, the galaxies would come towards each other again. At some stage the moment would then be reached at which all systems of stars would be grouped together at a single point. If we assume that this point in time really existed, then according to the standard model of cosmology it must have happened about 13.8 billion years ago.

Theoretical studies have been made of this moment, the birth of the universe. They state that all the material and radiation in the universe was compressed into a volume of just a few litres. In this state of concentrated mass and infinite heat, annihilation of elementary particles took place and an explosion, known as the Big Bang, happened. The resulting expansion led to a reduction of density and heat. The first elementary particles appeared. They formed a mixture of electrons (negatively charged particles),

Big Bang

Elementary Particles

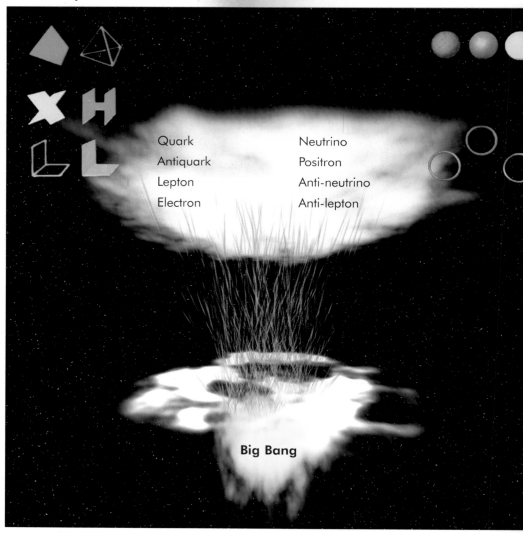

Quark

Antiquark

Lepton

Electron

Neutrino

Positron

Anti-neutrino

Anti-lepton

Big Bang

Elementary Particles

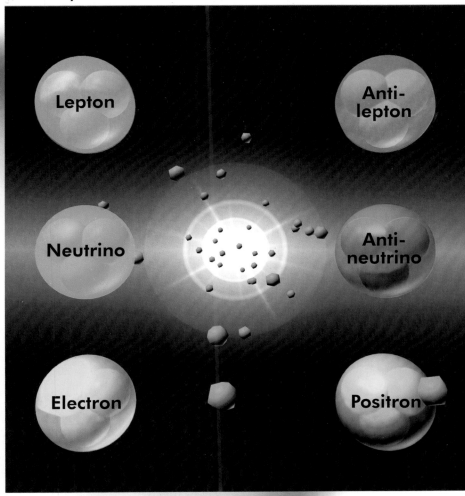

Big Bang
About 13.8 billion years ago the universe was in a state of infinite density and temperature. The Big Bang led to an explosive expansion and transformation that is continuing to this day.

neutrinos (neutral particles) and quarks (hypothetical elementary particles from which protons and neutrons are constituted), which were mingled with photons (particles of which radiation is composed). At the same time, in opposition to this matter, anti-matter was created. Anti-matter carries a charge with reversed polarity. Via the combination of quarks to make protons and neutrons, a mixture was formed of helium and hydrogen nuclei, electrons, photons and neutrinos.

During this process the universe continued to expand. The combination of electrons with hydrogen and helium nuclei finally laid the basis

for the formation of galaxies and stars.

The universe is not necessarily infinitely large. It has no limits, and yet it may have a finite volume. If we compare space with the surface of a sphere, we see that this surface is also without limits, and we can move in any direction and still return at some time to the starting point. The nature of three-dimensional space could be the same. We never reach a boundary, but we return to the starting point if we keep moving in the same direction. We then say that space has a positive curvature. In theory we ought to be able to see right around such a space, but this is not possible because it is expanding faster than light can travel around it.

Einstein's theory of relativity adds a fourth dimension to the curved space: time. This four-dimensional space-time continuum can only be expressed in mathematical terms. Even if we do not make the assumption that space is curved, we come up against a theoretical boundary.

Even objects that cannot yet be observed are not able to move away from us faster than the speed of light. One light year is the distance that light travels in a year at its speed of 300,000 km/s, approximately 30 million × 300,000 km = about 10,000 billion km. Under these conditions, galaxies moving at this speed could be a maximum of 13 billion light years distant. Have fun counting the noughts: 13 billion × 10 thousand billion!

The Origin of the Solar System

Solar nebula   Sun

The solar nebula continued to contract under the influence of gravity. The density was highest at its centre. This was the position of the sun, which now began to radiate light.

How did our sun and the planets come into existence? For centuries this question has occupied the minds of great scientists and philosophers. As long ago as the eighteenth century Immanuel Kant conjectured that our solar system was formed from a rotating cloud of dust and gas. Over the years repeated discoveries of clouds of gas and dust in the universe were made through telescopes, proving that space outside our solar system is not empty.

According to current thinking, the process probably took place as follows: about five billion years ago, enormous clouds of gas and dust particles were spinning through space. They formed the original solar nebula, as such a cloud is called. The force of gravity caused the nebula to contract further and further until it became a small, dense cloud.

Faster and faster spinning movements resulted in a flat disk of gas and dust. More and more matter flowed to the centre of this disk. Its density and temperature increased continually – up to an estimated 1,000,000 °C, causing the formation of a hot glowing body, the protosun. Processes of nuclear fusion began, similar to those in a hydrogen bomb: the high temperature and pressure forced hydrogen molecules together to form helium nuclei. We experience the energy released in this way as sunlight.

More matter was attracted by condensation, and protoplanets formed around the protosun. They grew and their gravitational attraction became stronger. By this means they attracted even more particles from the surrounding nebula.

As the solar nebula shrank, the protoplanets sucked in more and more matter from it. At first the solar system was not recognisable as such. The largest planets became larger and larger, while the number of smaller planets slowly decreased, so that only a few small bodies remained, spread out around the sun.

The Milky Way
Our solar system is situated in a galaxy consisting of a gigantic spiral of gas and billions of stars. The diameter of the whole galaxy is more than 100,000 light years.

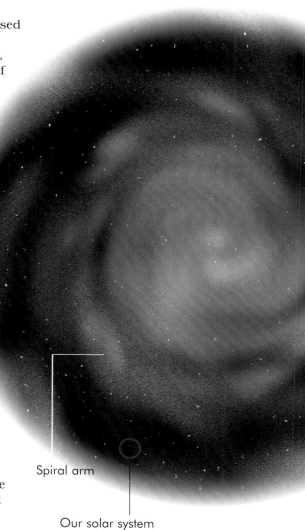

Spiral arm

Our solar system

Our Milky Way

On a clear, starry night it is possible to make out more than 3,000 stars with the naked eye. With one exception they all belong to the Milky Way, of which our solar system is a part. This one point of light that can be perceived outside the Milky Way is in reality a galaxy. It is the Andromeda galaxy.

With its billions of stars, our Milky Way looks like a shimmering ribbon in the sky, as the more distant stars cannot be individually seen. This ribbon also contains dark clouds of dust and shining clouds of gas (interstellar matter).

In order to express distances in the galaxy, researchers calculate in light years. One light year is the equivalent of 9.5 thousand billion kilometres. The galaxy where our solar system is located has a diameter of 100,000 light years. We are positioned 27,000 light years away from the centre of the galaxy.

The structure of the Milky Way can be derived from many observations of our galaxy and others: at the centre is a core with a vast number of stars. From this core several spiral arms wind out away from the centre. The solar system is located in one of these arms.

Large clouds of gas and dust are the production sites for new stars. These groups are known as open star clusters, because the stars, drawn by the gravitational force of other stars, gradually drift apart. In the outer reaches of the galaxy, up to a million stars come together to form a so-called globular star cluster. They revolve around the Milky Way system on elliptical orbits tilted at a large angle to the plane of the Milky Way. These stars were born in the early phase of galactic development, when the clouds of gas and dust had not been flattened as much as they are now.

As early as 1929 the American Edwin Hubble began to classify galaxies. He divided them into categories according to their geometrical features: elliptical, spiral and irregular systems.

Elliptical galaxies are clouds with an elliptical shape. Galaxies such as the Milky Way and the Andromeda nebula appear as flat disks surrounded by spiral arms. They are known as spiral galaxies. Irregular galaxies occur very seldom.

The variety of shapes of galaxies can be explained as follows: many galaxies were probably formed simultaneously, about two billion years after the birth of the universe. The galactic embryos consisting of hydrogen and helium contracted as a result of their own gravity, became denser and denser, and at some point in time fell apart into many billions of balls of gas.

Fig. 1–4
Our Milky Way, which is only a small part of the universe, belongs like the neighbouring Andromeda nebula to the category of spiral galaxies. As a result of the force of gravity, galaxies collect into galactic groups and galactic clusters.

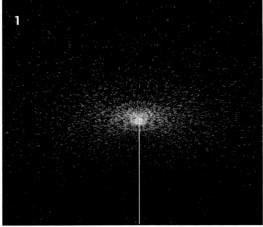
Elliptical galaxy

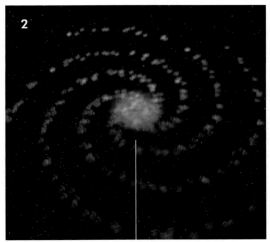
Spiral galaxy

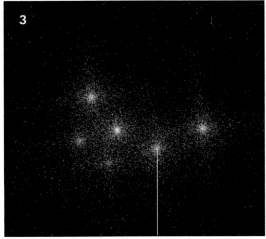
Irregular galaxy

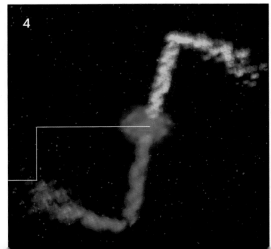
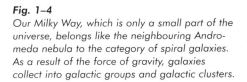
Barred spiral galaxy

Planets/Planetary Systems

What happened around the proto-sun? Scientists have worked out the following explanation: after the solar disc gradually cooled off, much of the matter swirling about it condensed to gas, ice and particles of radioactive dust, and formed other heavenly bodies (planetoids or protoplanets) which revolved around the sun. Through the force of gravity the heavenly bodies thus formed collided with each other again and again, and fused into larger objects.

As their size increased, so did their gravitational force, attracting more and more matter that made them grow until they had taken on a spherical shape as the planets of our solar system.

The sun now radiated energy as a result of thermonuclear activity. However, this process continued for a very long period.

The process of formation of the sun at the centre and the development of planets with their moons around the sun, the way we know the solar system today, happened about 4.6 billion years ago. Four inner planets were formed around the sun: Mercury, Venus, Earth and Mars. All of these consist of a core, a mantle and a crust.

The outer planets evolved at a greater distance: Jupiter, Saturn, Uranus and Neptune with their moons. They consist mainly of gases and ice.

Between the inner and outer planets are asteroids, the so-called minor planets or planetoids, which mainly consist of lumps of rock, and comets composed of ice, dust and rock. Every planet has its own orbit, on which it revolves around the sun.

Fig. 1–4
Condensations emerged around the sun and were able to attract more and more matter from the clouds surrounding them. The proto-planets formed in this way grew further and further by continually attracting matter, until finally about 4.6 billion years ago they had occupied the places in the solar system in which we find them today.

Formation of Planets

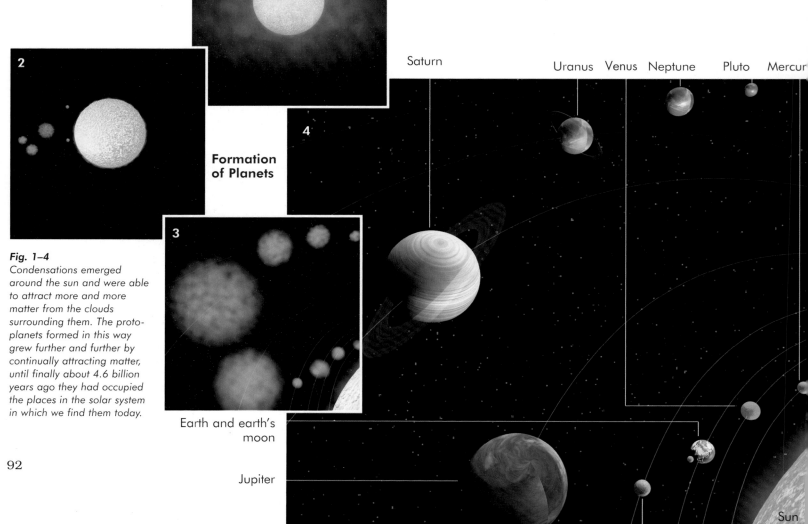

Earth and earth's moon

Jupiter

Mars

Saturn

Uranus Venus Neptune Pluto Mercur[y]

Sun

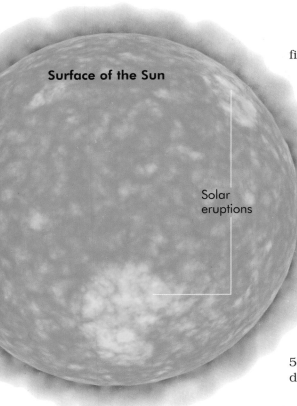

Surface of the Sun

Solar eruptions

Violent activity marks the surface of the sun. Gigantic eruptions and fires make it appear to be in constant movement.

The Sun

The sun played an important role for the great cultures of the past. Around 3.000 years ago in Egypt the sun was worshipped as the principal god. The Aztecs in Mexico and the Incas in Peru also had their cults of the sun, which often involved human sacrifices. In seventeenth-century France Louis XIV presented himself as the Sun King.

In 1543, for the first time, an astronomer provided proof that the planets revolve around the sun. The Polish astronomer Nicolaus Copernicus (1473–1543), whose main work "De revolutionibus orbium coelestium" ("On the revolutions of heavenly bodies") was not published until shortly before his death, believed that the planets move in a circular orbit and continued to adhere to the theory that there is a finite external sphere to which the fixed stars are attached. Johannes Kepler, a supporter of Copernicus, was the first to undertake the necessary corrections by describing the orbits as ellipses.

The sun is the basis for human life. It is our source of light and warmth. The sun rotates about its own axis once in about every 28 days. With a diameter of about 1.4 million km it is almost 110 times as large as the earth. 70% of the sun consists of hydrogen, 27% of helium. The temperature at the surface of the sun is about 5,700 °C and rises to several million degrees as the core is approached.

Atomic reactions take place in the sun's core. The nuclei of hydrogen atoms fuse after colliding and form helium nuclei. In the so-called radiation zone, energy is released in the form of radiation. It brings the matter in the adjacent convection zone into motion. Hot matter is passed on to the irregular solar surface. Cooler matter flows towards the centre. These motions within the matter cause eruptions on the sun's surface, which is known as the photosphere. Here there is continuous boiling of hot gases and powerful magnetic fields.

Cooler areas of the surface can be seen as dark spots, called sunspots. They were discovered as early as the seventeenth century. Parts of them, surrounded by a strong magnetic field, shoot thousands of kilometres into space. These colossal eruptions, which release enormous amounts of energy, are known as flares and prominences.

The sun's outer atmosphere is made up of thin veils of gas, the corona. During a solar eclipse, when the earth is positioned exactly in the shadow of the moon, it can be seen as a glowing ring around the darkened sun. An eclipse of the sun can only take place on a very small part of the earth, and lasts seven and a half minutes at the most. The space between the corona and the planets is filled with solar wind, which consists of electrically charged particles emitted by the sun.

Total Eclipse of the Sun

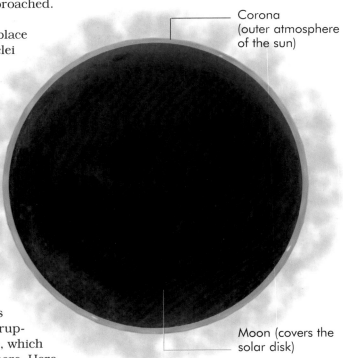

Corona (outer atmosphere of the sun)

Moon (covers the solar disk)

It has been calculated that the sun's hydrogen reserves will last for about another 5 billion years.

GLOSSARY

Abrasion
Wearing away of rocks by the action of the wind, water or glacier ice.

Arid
Dry, desert-like

Asthenosphere
Part of the earth's mantle, lying directly below the lithosphere at a depth of 100–300 km

Basalt
Fine-grained volcanic rock

Continental shelf
Area of shallow sea water on the edge of a continent

Convection currents
Movements of air, gas or liquids caused by the exchange between layers of different temperatures

Diffraction
The breaking up of a beam of light by a narrow opening or the edge of an object

Epicentre
The area directly above the point at which an earthquake originates

Equinox
The dates when the length of the night is equal to the length of the day: March 21 and September 23

Faraday cage
Electrical apparatus that shields its interior from an electric field, e. g. a car acts as a shield and protects its occupants from lightning

Fault
A break or discontinuity of the layers in a rock formation

Gabbro
A type of plutonic rock that has cooled slowly

Geyser
A hot spring that spouts steam and water

Glacier
A mass of ice flowing down a valley

Granite
Coarse-grained plutonic rock

Hot Spot
Place where hot lava flows from inside the earth

Hydrofluorocarbons
Substances used in aerosols, refrigerator and industry that contribute to the breakdown of the ozone layer

Lithosphere
Layer of rock comprising the earth's crust and the upper part of the earth's mantle

Magnitude
The amount by which the indicator of a measuring instrument moves

Mangroves
Plants that create new land by growing in the water

Metamorphic rock
Rock that has been transformed by heat and pressure

Mohorovicic discontinuity
A boundary layer between the earth's mantle and the earth's crust. Named after its discoverer, the Yugoslav seismologist Andrija Mohorovicic

Mollusc
Soft-bodied animals such as limpets, snails, oysters, mussels

Peridotite
A type of highly alkaline plutonic rock, and dominant rock of the upper part of the Earth's mantle

Photosynthesis
Transformation due to the effect of light. A biological process e. g. taking place in the leaves of plants

Plate boundaries
divergent = plates moving away from each other
convergent = plates moving towards each other
transform = plates sliding past each other

Precipitation
Water that falls to the ground in the form of rain, snow, hail, dew etc.

Protoplanet
Planet in its early or original form

Pumice
A light, spongy volcanic rock

Refraction
Bending of light

Sea-floor spreading
Formation of oceanic crust

Sediment
Rock that has been taken from its original position by the effect of the weather and deposited

Seismic waves
The pressure waves that spread out from the source of an earthquake

Solfataric field
An area where sulphurous gases are emitted from vents in the earth

Spectral colours
The colours of the rainbow

Subduction zones
Deep sea trenches where one continental plate slides under another

Tectonics
The structure of rocks or the earth's crust

Tsunamis
Gigantic waves that flood coastal areas

Viscous
Slow-flowing

INDEX

PICTURE CREDITS

Fotolia.com:
p. 6 Tungurahua eruption/© Ammit; p. 22 Seljalands-
foss waterfall in Iceland/© TTstudio; p. 50 lighting
over Caribbean Sea/© JM_Raggioli
NASA:
p. 34 atmosphere; p. 65 meteorite and meteorite
crater; p. 76 Blue Marble Western Hemisphere/Reto
Stöckli, based on data from NASA and NOAA, Instruments: Terra - MODIS; p. 78 earth and moon; p. 86
star cluster Westerlund 2/NASA, ESA and the Hubble
Heritage Team (STScl/AURA)
Wikimedia Commons:
p. 58 Aurora Borealis at Amundsen-Scott South Pole
Station/Chris Danals/National Science Foundation

All other illustrations: the contmedia GmbH archive